You're
Losing Us

You're Losing Us

Connecting Your Faith to a New Generation

Everett Leadingham

*Tell it to your children,
and let your children tell it to their children,
and their children to the next generation*
(Joel 1:3).

Though this book is designed for group study, it is also intended for
personal enjoyment and spiritual growth. A leader's guide is available
from your local bookstore or your publisher.

Beacon Hill Press of Kansas City
Kansas City, Missouri

ISBN: 083-411-9978

Printed in the United States of America

Editor: Everett Leadingham
Associate Editor: Charlie L. Yourdon
Executive Editor: Larry R. Morris
Writer: Everett Leadingham

Cover Design: Kevin Williamson
Cover Photo: Don Pluff

10   9   8   7   6   5   4   3   2

Contents

1. The Future in a Basket — 9

2. Generation to Generation — 17

3. Keeping the Faith — 25

4. Who We Are — 35

5. Being the Church — 43

6. Matching Words and Actions — 51

7. Revival or Survival? — 61

8. Faith Begins at Home — 69

9. Family Is a Verb — 79

10. Starting Over — 89

11. Telling the Story — 99

12. The Faces Around Us — 109

13. Let's Do Something! — 1

Meet the Christians

At the beginning of each chapter in this book, we will learn a little more about this fictional family.

The family consists of Grandma and Grandpa Christian, the rock-solid believers who raised their children in the faith. Bob Christian, their son, is married to Betty. Together they are the concerned parents, raising three children in today's tumultuous times. Their three children are 15-year-old Bobby, 12-year-old Mary, and 10-year-old Kevin. Each child has his or her own perspective on life, as we will see.

We hope that watching the Christian family wrestle with important issues will help us understand how to better pass on the faith to our own next generation.

A Glimpse of the Real World

It had been a pleasant day at Grandpa and Grandma Christian's house. Bob and Betty Christian, along with their three children, had spent the afternoon eating Grandpa's great barbecue and listening to Grandma talk about "the good ol' days."

Now it was time to go home. As they backed out of the driveway, Bobby exclaimed, "I'm glad that's over with!"

Shocked, Bob asked what he meant.

"Oh, Grandma goes on and on about the old days. I get tired of hearing about her old ways. She's way out of it with her old-fashioned beliefs about God."

"You don't believe in God?" Betty asked, trying to keep the panic out of her voice.

"Sure, I believe in God. I just don't believe everything Grandma does. Why should I? She can believe what she wants to, and I can believe what I think is right."

Bob and Betty looked at each other. Bob whispered, "What has happened to his faith?" Betty's anguished look showed she agreed on the unspoken question: *Will Christianity survive in the next generation with attitudes like that?*

1

The Future in a Basket

PHARAOH FELT threatened. At the rate the Hebrew slaves were multiplying, he was afraid that Egypt would be overrun with them in the next generation. So, he reacted to the situation with a new policy: "Drown all the Hebrew baby boys."

That sounds harsh to us, but he wanted to stop the next generation. And throwing all the babies into the river would do just that.

Next generations are at risk all the time. It doesn't take something as drastic as an executive order for murder to keep the next generation from inheriting all it should from the present one. It only takes neglect. It's a bit like the old saying about health: "Ignore it and it will go away." If neglected, Christianity is only one generation away from extinction.

Pharaoh was not successful at eliminating the Hebrew threat. It only took the actions of one person to thwart his plan and bring about God's will for the Hebrew people.

Moses' mother hid him for three months after he was born. Then she made him a little boat out of a basket waterproofed with tar. She set the boat adrift at the edge of the Nile and had Moses' sister keep her eye on it. When the Pharaoh's daughter rescued the baby from the water, Moses' sister offered to "get one of the Hebrew women to nurse the baby for" her (Exodus 2:7).

Of course, she got Moses' mother, and Pharaoh's daughter even paid her to take care of her own son.

Will the Church Survive to the Next Generation?

How important that basket was to Moses' life and to the Israelite nation! His mother recognized the danger to the next generation in Pharaoh's decree, and she constructed a waterproof haven to protect Moses and ensure the future.

As Christians, we are faced with a question similar to Moses' mother's dilemma: Will the Church survive to the next generation? Though no one has issued a decree to drown all Christians, there are trends that are increasingly alarming.

For example, church attendance is declining. According to a recent study done by a major university, church attendance in the United States went from 60 percent in 1981 to 55 percent in 1998. And that was based on respondents saying they went to church at least once a month![1]

The question is: How can we build a "basket" that will be a safe haven for the next generation and ensure that the Christian faith will be alive and well in the future? That's what we want to examine from several different angles in this book. We want to hear the plaintive cry of our children, "You're losing us," and do something constructive about it.

The Perils in Our Culture

What perils are in the culture surrounding Christianity that will affect the present generation as well as the next one? What factors exist that, if left unchallenged, might spell the end of Christianity in the next decade?

Two realities in society have a potential deadly effect on the next generation. Each has a spiritual problem at its root, and both can impact our children.

Physical dangers. Our culture seems to be more violent than it used to be. A rash of school shootings has been in the news in the past few years. Some of those shootings have even occurred in churches. Youth no longer settle differences of opinion with words or fists; now they use deadly weapons, like knives and guns. An FBI report for 92 selected cities in the United States reported 5,976 murders in 1999.[2] We wonder, how many of those were children fighting other children?

Suicide among 15- to 24-year-olds is also an alarming display of violence. "About every two hours a young person in the United States between the ages of 15 and 24 dies of suicide. . . . Suicide is the second-leading cause of death for college students (after accidents), and the third-leading cause of death (after accidents and homicides) for all those 15-24."[3]

Our culture seems to have a growing problem with alcohol and drug abuse as well. Alcohol-related deaths top 100,000 each year,[4] and some experts feel the reality may be closer to six times that number. A British doctor summed up the impact in this way: "I cannot underestimate the importance of alcohol in the workload of emergency departments. We would be out of business if it was not for alcohol."[5]

What is missing in the lives of people today that they turn violent to express themselves and turn to alcohol and illegal drugs to try to escape their pain? What spiritual direction are they lacking? Are we, as Christians, doing all we can to make a positive impact on their lives?

Spiritual dangers. The evidence shows that there are so many choices about spirituality in the open marketplace of ideas that Christianity is losing its prominence. Our society has accepted two ideas that weaken the influence of the Church today.

First, many (if not most) people ascribe to the idea that personal preference is the final judge of what is true or good. They live by the philosophy "My viewpoint is the only thing valid for me; *your* view is valid for you." Such persons do not look beyond themselves for a foundation of truth. Brought into the Church, this idea is divisive, because often the number of different opinions equals the number of persons in a room. How can we "make every effort to keep the unity of the Spirit through the bond of peace" (Ephesians 4:3) if we listen only to ourselves rather than God's truth?

The other idea of pluralism that impacts the Church today is that all roads lead equally well to God. That sounds like a pleasant statement ensuring equality and tolerance, and we want to be fair to all and tolerant of differences. Yet, Jesus said clearly, "I am the way and the truth and the life. *No one comes to the Father except through me*" (John 14:6, emphasis added).

Inadequate or Inappropriate Responses

When we look around at the violence that threatens the lives of our children and see the ideas that are eroding Christianity, how do we react?

Some people react with fear. They develop a bunker mentality and cut off all contact with the world outside their particular corner of the Christian Church. Such persons find a comforting directive in the words "Therefore come out from them and be separate, says the Lord" (2 Corinthians 6:17).

Some other people react with despair. They watch the news and see how bad the situation has become; then they feel overwhelmed. They give up, saying, "There's nothing we can do."

Another way to respond is through accommodation. This can happen in a negative way or a positive one. On the downside, we can ignore the changes, which are usually subtle and gradual, until things have changed so much that we cannot tell the difference between what we believe and what the world believes. In this way, it becomes impossible to answer the question: Does the Church shape the culture, or does the culture shape the Church?

On the upside, we can see how things are shaping up in society and find new ways to share the gospel. The content of the message never changes, but the package it's shipped in must constantly adjust if the truth of Christianity is to be received and accepted by a confused world. Packaging the uncompromising message in ways that totally secular people can hear the truth of the gospel is effective evangelism.

What Is Our Hope and Our Goal?

Why do we want to protect our values and pass our faith on to the next generation? Because we want them to be Christians in the future. We desire that the saving power of Jesus that has been real in our lives will become a reality in theirs.

Why does this task seem so difficult? After all, isn't God in control? Doesn't the Holy Spirit lead and protect? Yes, of course. However, in the day-to-day grind of living, the secular culture seems to dominate nearly everything around us. If only 55 percent of Americans are churchgoers, and only once a month at that, secularism does indeed rule at least half of our society. And the voices of the media are so loud, it can seem as if they dominate 90 percent.

Before we throw our hands up in despair, however, let us remember Moses' story. His mother was a rebel; she went against the dominant culture to save Moses in the midst of that culture. He was reared in an Egyptian palace, taught in an Egyptian school, dressed like an Egyptian prince, and probably even walked like an Egyptian. Yet, thanks to his mother, in his heart he was a Hebrew! She instilled the values of the Hebrew faith in him that helped him understand and respond to the call from the burning bush 80 years later (see Acts 7:17-36).

What Is Our Plan?

Our task is to construct a basket and make it leakproof. We need to find ways to pass on our faith to the next generation while they are forced to swim in the shark-infested waters of the present. Moses' story is about a parent who did all she could to prepare her child to face the hostile world that would soon engulf him. That is our task as well.

The early years of a child's life are extremely important in molding values and setting priorities. Yet, all is not lost with older children. Studies show that family continues to be the major influence on children and teens. Thus, we have ads urging parents to talk to their kids about drugs. We need to continue talking to them about our Christian faith too. We can start at any age; only the methods needed to reach them may be different.

We need to pass on our faith in a myriad of ways. We can take our cues from the apostle Paul's method: "I have become all things to all men *so that by all possible means I might save some*" (1 Corinthians 9:22, emphasis added).

When our time on earth is over, when we have passed the torch to the next generation, we want to be able to say what Paul proclaimed near the end of his life: "I have finished the race, I have kept the faith" (2 Timothy 4:7).

Everyone Is Important

There is no way to know what is wrapped up in a child. We have no way of knowing whom God will call to a significant ministry or place of dedicated service. Yet, all children are special, and God has an important place in His kingdom for each one.

The story is told of a man who, on his way to church one day, noticed four boys loitering on the corner. He invited them to church and organized a new Sunday School class for them. Many years later, the boys scattered into adulthood.

In 1932, on the man's birthday, he received letters from each of those four boys. One was a missionary in China. Another was the president of the Federal Reserve Bank. A third was the private secretary to President Herbert Hoover. And the fourth was President Hoover himself.

You never know what's wrapped up in a child! That's what can make passing on our faith so exciting.

Notes:

1. "Church Attendance Drops," news release from the University of Michigan, <www.umich.edu/~newsinfo>, January 11, 2000.

2. "Murders in U.S. Cities," <www.govspot.com/lists/murder.htm>, March 12, 2002.

3. "Dying Young," *Christian Century*, March 13-20, 2002, 5.

4. "Number of Deaths and Age-Adjusted Death Rates per 100,000 Population for Categories of Alcohol-Related (A-R) Mortality, United States and

States, 1979-1996," <www.alcoholism.about.com/library/narmort01.htm>, April 16, 2002.

5. John Ryan, quoted in "Huge Rise in Alcohol-Related Deaths," BBC News, <www.news.bbc.co.uk>, May 10, 2000.

Scripture: Exodus 1:22—2:10; John 14:6; Acts 7:17-36; 1 Corinthians 9:22; 2 Corinthians 6:17; Ephesians 4:3; 2 Timothy 4:7

A Glimpse of the Real World

Kevin Christian and his dad, Bob, were walking out of the church one Sunday morning. An elderly gentleman, a longtime member of Pleasant Street Church, smiled at them and wished them, "Good day."

As the man walked away, Kevin said, "I don't like that old man."

Bob reprimanded him. "Kevin! You shouldn't say a thing like that. Have respect for your elders."

"He's mean," Kevin responded. "He's always yelling at us kids to be quiet or stop running in the church. He never smiles at us; he's only nice to grown-ups. I don't want to be like him when I grow up!"

Bob felt his heart sink as he wondered, *Will anyone at this church be a good spiritual model for my children?*

2

Generation to Generation

A YOUNG MOTHER was sewing while her toddler daughter played nearby. Totally involved, she was unaware that her daughter had joined her by the sewing machine. She looked up to see her two-year-old's mouth lined with straight pins. Her immediate impulse was to grab the pins away and scold the youngster. However, when she tried to speak, she suddenly realized her own mouth was lined with pins, a habitual and unconscious sewing practice.

Instead of scolding, the mother pulled the pins from her own mouth. Replacing them in the pincushion, she said, "Mommy has done a very dangerous thing. We must never place pins in our mouths." The toddler immediately followed suit, imitating her mother's positive action as easily and automatically as she had the negative one.

This mother's example is a good illustration of the influence we have over our children. Such a mother would eventually teach her daughter to sew. Then remembering the lessons her mother taught her, the daughter would teach her daughter—or son—to sew. As each successive generation sewed, they would probably often say, "Here's how my grandmother did it."

The Christian faith follows the same principle. It passes from generation to generation by example. As the prophet Joel encouraged, "Tell it to your children, and let your children tell it to their children, and their children to the next generation" (1:3).

Passing on the Faith Old Testament Style

Whether gathered around the supper table, a warm hearth on cold evenings, or a festival dinner, the Jewish children heard the stories of their people. Since the time of Moses, retelling the events of the Exodus and talking about Israel's faith in God had been priorities for the Jews. The ancestors even left physical reminders to assist parents in the process of instructing the young ones.

When Joshua led the people across the Jordan River into the Promised Land after Moses' death, the occasion was marked with stones from the river bottom. As the people passed through on dry ground, they were reminded of the escape through the Red Sea. Twelve stones, one representing each tribe, were carried out of the riverbed and set up on the bank as a memorial. Whenever the children saw the stone monument and asked, they heard the story of the river crossing again.

As they entered their houses, they saw a reminder as well. A small container, called a mezuzah, hung on the doorframe of every Jewish house. Inside the small case were these words: "Hear, O Israel: The Lord our God, the Lord is one. Love the Lord your God with all your heart and with all your soul and with all your strength" (Deuteronomy 6:4-5). This was to remind the Hebrews to do what Moses had told them: "These commandments that I give you today are to be upon your hearts. Impress them on your children. Talk about them when you sit at home and when you walk along the road, when you lie down and when you get up" (vv. 6-7).

Even today, when families gather to celebrate the annual Passover meal, the story of freedom from Egyptian bondage is repeated. In the ceremony, the children have questions to ask, and the answers to those questions instruct them in the stories of their people.

Faith in Three Generations

The path of faith is always made smoother by the examples of godly people. In the New Testament, Timothy was already a third-generation Christian, though only about 30 years had passed since Jesus' death and resurrection. The same "sincere faith" (2 Timothy 1:5) Paul saw in Timothy he also had seen in Timothy's grandmother Lois and his mother Eunice.

Paul himself came from a long line of persons of faith, though all his ancestors had been Jews rather than Christians. Still, probably quite unintentionally, they had an influence on Paul in the matter of his Christian faith. His heritage had made him a highly zealous religious person. In his zeal, Paul began to persecute the fledgling Christian Church. His actions put him directly in the path to be miraculously converted to being a follower of Jesus. Then he could still claim his spiritual heritage by saying to Timothy, "I thank God, whom I serve, as my forefathers did, with a clear conscience" (2 Timothy 1:3).

The Power of Influence

Paul could trace his religious roots back several generations. Two godly women who were of different generations had influenced Timothy. We, too, have a number of good examples of people who have shaped our faith. Hopefully, it is a large number. Somewhere among the parents and grandparents, the Sunday School teachers and pastors, or the other relatives and good friends are some persons who told us the story of Jesus and lived Christlike lives in front of us. They made the gospel a living show-and-tell event.

One of those influential persons in my life was Joe, the pastor who finally convinced me to follow God's call on my life and attend seminary. Joe often said that, as Christians, we need to be "tough-minded and tenderhearted." By that, he meant that we have an obligation to learn all we can from the Bible and the study of theology so that we can "be prepared to give an answer to everyone who asks [us] to give the reason for the hope that

[we] have" (1 Peter 3:15). We need to be tough-minded when it comes to defending the Christian faith.

At the same time, we must never let what we know make us think we are better than other people. We still must be emotionally available to them. We need to cry when they cry and laugh when they laugh. Our involvement in other people's lives should be no less than that of Jesus, who "when he saw the crowds, . . . had compassion on them, because they were harassed and helpless, like sheep without a shepherd" (Matthew 9:36).

Joe lived out his "tough-minded, tenderhearted" philosophy in front of us every day. His influence inspired me to say more than once about my Christian faith, "I want to be like Joe." And to this day I haven't seen a more Christlike example than his.

The other side of the coin is possible as well. Some people, by their bad examples, lead persons away from the church and from God. Some intentionally rail against the church and Christianity, as if those are bad things. Others are subtle, even unintentional, bad influences. Like gossiping about other Christians, which leaves a bad impression on impressionable persons. Or like skipping Sunday School or worship when something else more "fun" is available to do. The list can be long, and you can fill in plenty of other illustrations for yourself.

Being a Good Influence Takes Commitment

The critical question for us and for this book is, How can we make a difference? The answer sounds simple: We must decide to be good examples. Throughout our Christian lives, we must constantly make decisions, and those actions will reflect what kind of influence we have on others. We must remain determined to serve Christ, regardless of what others around us are doing.

History reveals that the decision to follow the Lord is not made lightly nor kept easily. Such an important commitment does not happen haphazardly or by accident. It always must be an intentional conclusion.

Despite the fact that Moses had instructed the people to

constantly remind themselves of their relationship to God and His law, over the years they slipped away from their devotion. They neglected their worship practices and became entangled with the false gods of foreigners. When they insisted on having an earthly king, they turned further away from God. Over the years, even the books that held the Law were lost.

When the lost Book of the Law was rediscovered in the Temple, King Josiah gathered the Israelite people in Jerusalem. He read for them all the words of the book. Then he did something intentional. "The king stood by the pillar and renewed the covenant in the presence of the LORD—to follow the LORD and keep his commands, regulations and decrees with all his heart and all his soul." Following the king's example, "All the people pledged themselves to the covenant" (2 Kings 23:3).

God expected nothing less than the entire devotion of the Israelites. Such total commitment was also anticipated in the New Testament.

It cost something to follow Jesus. He did not lightly invite persons to follow Him. One man wanted to delay his discipleship until after his father was dead and buried. "But Jesus told him, 'Follow me, and let the dead bury their own dead'" (Matthew 8:22). When Jesus called Matthew away from his tax collection business, he immediately left everything to go with Jesus (see 9:9).

In another instance, Jesus said, "Anyone who loves his father or mother more than me is not worthy of me; anyone who loves his son or daughter more than me is not worthy of me; and anyone who does not take his cross and follow me is not worthy of me" (10:37-38). On a different occasion, He repeated himself so that the disciples would know exactly what following Him means. "If anyone would come after me, he must deny himself and take up his cross and follow me. For whoever wants to save his life will lose it, but whoever loses his life for me will find it" (16:24-25).

If that does not make it clear that nothing less than total devotion was necessary, listen to how Jesus explained it to the rich young man. "Go, sell your possessions and give to the poor, and you will have treasure in heaven. Then come, follow me" (19:21).

Every business deal, every family relationship, everything we own must all become second (or third or even last) place to our devotion to Christ. Though our secular culture doesn't understand it, choosing to follow Jesus is a good decision, the best one, the only really worthwhile one. It is worth everything we might have to give up in order to be completely His, because we can rely on Jesus. He is completely consistent and eternal. "Jesus Christ is the same yesterday and today and forever" (Hebrews 13:8).

Being a Good Influence Is Worth It

Every time we decide to take a path that leads us toward God, and thereby shun a trail that leads away from Him, we potentially influence someone to do the same. Other Christians are watching us to see how we follow Christ. Our children are watching us, looking for a consistency that tells them the Christian faith means something to us and will be worth their time.

We decide, by our actions and our intentions, to be good examples to those over whom we have some influence. The example we set is important because God can use it to draw others to himself.

The Christian faith will continue to be strong as each generation influences the next one for the Lord. When we see those who come after us making commitments to serve God wholeheartedly, we will be able to share what should be the best news a Christian can hear. As John wrote to his friend Gaius, "It gave me great joy to have some brothers come and tell about your faithfulness to the truth and how you continue to walk in the truth. *I have no greater joy than to hear that my children are walking in the truth*" (3 John 3-4, emphasis added).

May God help us to make the right decisions and continue to influence the next generation to walk in the truth.

Scripture: Deuteronomy 6:4-7; 2 Kings 23:3; Joel 1:3; Matthew 8:22; 9:9, 36; 10:37-38; 16:24-25; 19:21; 2 Timothy 1:3-5; Hebrews 13:8; 1 Peter 3:15; 3 John 3-4

A Glimpse of the Real World

Betty was driving Mary to soccer practice. Mary, who had been thinking about what her brother had said about their grandma's old-fashioned beliefs, asked, "Mom, tell me what church was like when you were a girl."

"Well," Betty started, "it was a lot different back then. Stricter. There were a lot more rules."

"What kind of rules?"

"Well, we couldn't wear certain kinds of clothes, like shorts or blue jeans. We weren't allowed to eat in restaurants on Sunday. We couldn't play certain games or watch some programs on TV. And we always had to go to church and Sunday School on Sunday morning, attend Sunday night service, and be at midweek prayer meeting—even if we had homework to do."

"No shorts!" Mary exclaimed. "Weren't you hot in the summer?"

"Of course, but we managed to survive."

"We had Grandpa's birthday dinner at a restaurant last Sunday. Isn't that against the rules? Don't you believe those things anymore?"

Betty sighed. *Have my beliefs changed?* she wondered. *And how do I explain what we still believe to a 12-year-old?*

3

Keeping the Faith

IT WAS A TYPICAL Easter Sunday.

The alarm went off about an hour before daylight. The whole family arose and sleepily prepared to go to church. We put on our new clothes. I wore a light-colored suit; it was gray. My wife and daughter put on matching pastel green dress outfits, complete with white shoes, white gloves, and flower-bedecked, lacy, wide-brimmed straw hats.

We piled into the car, and off we went to the city park. There we participated in the community sunrise service. We sang Easter hymns as the sun rose over the beautiful trees. The pastor prayed and preached, surrounded by freshly blooming flowers.

When the service ended, we piled back in the car and drove to our church. We shared a scrambled-egg-and-sausage breakfast with our good friends. Then we stayed for Sunday School and a majestic Easter worship service.

Around noon, in the car again, we headed to Grandpa and Grandma's house for dinner. Once there, all the children of the family found Easter baskets full of candy, "left by the Easter bunny," according to Grandma. Then the cousins joined in looking for colored hard-boiled eggs on the lawn. Finally, we all gathered around the large table—Grandma and Grandpa, brothers and sisters, aunts and uncles, and cousins—for a big ham dinner, with all the trimmings. After we were so full we could hardly walk, we lazed around in the living room, talking, laughing, and having a good time just being together.

It was a typical Easter Sunday because it was full of familiar traditions.

As I think back on that occasion, I begin to wonder. How much of what we did that day truly belongs to a Christian celebration of the Resurrection? How much of it have Christians adapted from pagan customs? How much of these traditions should we keep; how much discard? And most important, how can we know the best answers to these questions?

First, let's take a little tour "around Robin Hood's barn." Maybe when we return, we will have found the answers to our questions.

The Jews Celebrate Passover

Exodus 12 describes for the first time a meal that would become an annual festival, which is still celebrated today. In this chapter, God explained to Moses and Aaron how the Israelites were to prepare for their last night in Egyptian slavery.

Each household was to prepare a meal of roasted lamb, bitter herbs, and bread without yeast. They were to eat the meal hurriedly, dressed in their traveling clothes. Furthermore, when each lamb was killed, a small portion of its blood was to be painted on the doorframes of their houses. God's angel of death would then pass over every Israelite house that had blood showing on the door. Only the unmarked Egyptian households would lose the eldest child to death on that night.

Though this was an important night for the Hebrews (their freedom was a few scant hours away), this Passover meal was not a one-time-only affair. From that time until now, it has been an important point for Jews to remember how God freed them from slavery and led them to the Promised Land. It remains a symbol of the future reestablishment of the Messiah's kingdom at the end of time.

The Passover meal is important to Christians, too, though we may not recognize it because we now call it "the Lord's Supper." Jesus was sharing the Passover meal with His disciples in an upper room when He applied the meaning of the bread and wine to himself.

The apostle Paul made the connection clear for the Christians at Corinth. He challenged them to a new level of holy living through the Lord's Supper, to break away from the old bondage and move toward a new freedom (1 Corinthians 5:7-8). Then Paul made it perfectly clear to the Corinthians that celebrating the Lord's Supper proclaims this good news until Jesus returns (11:26).

Regular celebrations are an important way to pass on the faith from one generation to the next. This is one of the reasons we gather Sunday after Sunday to worship. This is the value of the holy days, like Easter and Christmas. This is why family worship rituals and traditions are so necessary.

Though traditions are an important way to pass on the Christian faith, most are not always clearly Christian. As we saw at the beginning of this chapter, Easter has become a mixture of sacred and secular symbols. Therefore, every Christian family must ask itself an important question.

What Traditions Do We Celebrate?

Easter is not the only holiday that has become a mixture of traditions for Christian families. Our culture has affected the way we celebrate Christmas too. The top priority now seems to be making sure all the necessary gifts have been purchased. The list of "necessary" gifts can get quite long, as we are encouraged to buy for everyone from our closest relatives to the service person we see only occasionally during the year. The stores often try to help us in this task by displaying their Christmas wares as early as September.

As Christmas Day gets closer, we see and hear how the culture wants us to celebrate the season. In fact, we bump into their not-so-subtle message everywhere we turn. How can we sort through all these holiday traditions and keep the ones with spiritual importance? Which of the things we do reflect the true good news of Christmas, that God sent His Son as a baby to redeem us from sin?

And what about other holidays? The calendar year is full of them. Do we as Christians look for connections to the sacred in other holidays, or do we simply write them off as purely secular?

Some Things We Can Do

Do we take secular holidays as opportunities to reflect on God's grace? Think about the annual celebration of birthdays. Are they simply about ice cream and cake, jokes about aging, and receiving presents? Or could they also be occasions for our families to talk about the many ways God has been present in our lives in the past year?

Annual holidays are not the only place we can look to see cultural and Christian traditions mixed. Sunday rolls around every week. How do we, as Christians, use our time on Sunday? Is church and Sunday School an interruption in our busy schedule, or the weekly highlight in the practice of our faith? Do we feel obligated to "give" God so many hours on Sunday, but the rest of the day is ours to do with as we please? Does our use of time on the Sabbath suggest that God is the essential part of our family's life and reflect that we want to honor Him in all we do? These are important questions each Christian family needs to consider.

Easter, Christmas, other annual holidays, and even the Lord's day have all been overgrown with human practices. Which of these customs have obscured the Christian message for our families? Which of these have helped our families grow in their Christian faith? How do we sort out the harmful ways from the helpful ones? The answer is simple, but not easy. We must examine all of what we do and see how each practice lines up with the basics of the Christian faith.

That immediately brings us to another key question.

What Are the Basics?

When we strip away the layers of human tradition that have been laid on Christian beliefs over the centuries, what will we find as the core of basic beliefs? Paul helped us answer this question in 1 Corinthians 15. He boiled the essence of the gospel down to three points:

- "Christ died for our sins" (v. 3).
- "He was buried" (v. 4*a*).
- "He was raised on the third day" (v. 4*b*).

Christ's death and resurrection are the essential and unique message of Christianity. Jesus' death atoned for the sins of humanity, and His resurrection conquered death. And both events happened for our benefit. Both are a clear message of God's great love for humanity. "For God so loved the world that he gave his one and only Son, that whoever believes in him shall not perish but have eternal life" (John 3:16).

Mixed-up Counterfeits

Just about everything genuine has a counterfeit. We can buy watches that look exactly like Rolexes for a few dollars rather than a few thousand dollars. We can obtain college degrees from "diploma mills" by paying a few bucks and without going to classes. Hanging on the wall, they look just like the ones people spend four arduous years earning. Name anything that is expensive or genuine, and someone can probably get you a cheap copy of it.

C. S. Lewis gave us a good insight about counterfeits. He said that we know the reality by observing the forgeries. There has to be a genuine article for a counterfeit to be possible. No one "knocks off" a copy of something that does not exist. Therefore, belief in the existence of false gods points to the reality of the true God.

The essence of the gospel doesn't always get communicated clearly to every generation. Often the counterfeit ideas are mistaken for the truth. Many times human ideas overlay the true message so much that it gets buried and nearly lost.

For example, the three basic beliefs mentioned above are the straightforward message of the gospel. However, they have been mixed up in so many ways, some people never hear them clearly. Have you ever heard anyone spout any of the following ideas?

- Christ died for our sins, but we still have to pay our own penance, either in this life or in a purging place of fire after death, before we can go to heaven.
- Christ's sacrificial death was only effective for a preselected number of people. The rest will be lost.
- Christ only *appeared* to die. Actually, He swooned on the Cross and woke up in the tomb on Sunday.
- Christ was not really raised from the dead. The disciples stole His body and lied to us.

Sorting Through the Distortions

How can we sort through these and many other distortions of the gospel? How can we find the truth of the faith we want to pass along to the next generation? It takes effort. It takes time. Yet, it is possible if we will pay attention to several ways God helps us.

The Holy Spirit: Listening to the Holy Spirit is the starting point. Jesus promised His disciples, "When he, the Spirit of truth, comes, he will guide you into all truth" (John 16:13). The promise still holds true for Christians today.

The Bible: Reading is fundamental to finding out what we believe. The time we spend reading the Bible is never wasted. As the Holy Spirit illuminates the meaning of texts, we learn. We learn the facts of the Bible as well as the message of the words.

Christian Community: There is no substitute for reading the sacred texts, but we need also to read solid commentaries. The theologians who devote their lives to study of the Word help us understand things about Scripture that we would never stumble onto on our own. Also, commentaries can help us get in touch with how the Church has traditionally understood particular texts down through the centuries.

Informed discussion within our church groups will also help us understand the message of the gospel clearly. The prayers and insights of other Christians within a faith community strengthen the faith of us all.

Our Hearts: Finally, we need to carefully consider our intuitions, our "gut feelings." They can be a part of the process in discerning the truth. In that way we may sense the Holy Spirit's leading. John gave us both an encouragement and a warning in this matter: "Do not believe every spirit, but test the spirits to see whether they are from God, because many false prophets have gone out into the world. This is how you can recognize the Spirit of God: Every spirit that acknowledges that Jesus Christ has come in the flesh is from God, but every spirit that does not acknowledge Jesus is not from God" (1 John 4:1-3).

Reaching the Right Conclusions

Well, we are rounding the last corner of the process. Up ahead we can see again the "typical Easter" scene that opened this chapter. Are the answers to the questions becoming clear?

The celebration we know as Easter started long before Jesus came to earth. The pagans believed in a goddess of spring named Oestre (or Eostre). They held festivals every year in her honor to herald the arrival of spring after winter's long, cold months.[1] Though the term is not biblical, Christians adapted the goddess's name into "Easter" and changed the focus to a celebration of Jesus' resurrection. This is typical of other pagan holidays Christians transformed. Christmas became the Christian alternative to the pagan observance of the feast to the sun god, Mithras. And its December 25 date came about by refocusing from the festival held on that date honoring the mythical god Saturn to the birth of Christ.[2]

Usually the pagan spring festival started at sunrise after the vernal equinox (the day in spring when the shorter daylight hours of winter give way to 12 hours of darkness and 12 hours of light). Christians, thinking about the story of the women going to Christ's empty tomb at dawn, adapted the sunrise celebration to begin Easter. "All over the Christian world people have gathered on hilltops, beaches, and open meadows to greet the rising sun, the visual reminder of the 'Risen Son of God.'" However, it was not until 1732 that greeting the rising sun turned into a sunrise service. Moravian settlers brought the idea with them to America in the colonial days, and the practice is alive and well today.[3]

Rabbits and Easter eggs probably came from pagan practice as well. The traditional symbols for the goddess Oestre were the hare and the egg.[4] That is probably the origin of the Easter bunny, which Christians did not adapt to their use. However, they did give new meaning to the egg as "a symbol of the tomb out of which Christ reappeared in newness of life."[5]

The idea of wearing new clothes in the spring may have been around before Easter celebrations began. However, "New clothes have been understood by many Christians to symbolize the righteousness that comes from God and the new life we have because of the Resurrection."[6]

That only leaves us two unexplained Easter traditions that my family observed—attending Sunday School and church and the family dinner. Church attendance is part of the weekly practice as the faith community gathers to learn about God and to worship Him. Easter Sunday is a special observance of that weekly practice, because Easter reminds us of the unique foundation of our Christian hope—the empty tomb.

The family dinner? I don't know. I guess we just enjoy gathering together as a family and sharing a delicious and happy meal. Easter is as good an "excuse" as any other holiday.

When the folks gather around the dinner table next Easter, how can we pass on the true story? We can look at each symbol of Easter—the new clothes, the colored eggs, the Easter bunny, and all the rest—and ask this question: Can anyone explain how each item relates to the resurrection of Christ? If they cannot find a direct connection, perhaps the tradition should be dropped.

Ouch! If I follow this advice, there go my favorites—the jelly beans. As good as they taste, jelly beans do not remind us of the sacrificial death and glorious resurrection of our Lord. And it is only the true faith we want to keep and pass on to our children.

Notes:

1. Richard Patterson Jr., "Who's Afraid of the Big Bad Easter Bunny?" *The Outlook* (March 31, 2002), 8.

2. *To Celebrate: Reshaping Holidays and Rites of Passage* (Ellenwood, Ga.: Alternatives, 1987), 28.

3. Martha Zimmerman, *Celebrating the Christian Year* (Minneapolis: Bethany House Publishers, 1993), 152.

4. *To Celebrate*, 101.

5. Zimmerman, *Celebrating the Christian Year*, 153.

6. Patterson, "Who's Afraid?" 9.

Scripture: Exodus 12; John 3:16; 16:13; 1 Corinthians 5:7-8; 11:26; 15:3-4; 1 John 4:1-3

A Glimpse of the Real World

Pleasant Street Church was kind of small. The church across town was big.

Bob decided to move his family to the big church to try it out. "I think my family needs the variety of programs our church just can't offer." It wasn't long until Bob felt that the big church was the right place for his family to be. Everything about the big church across town was exciting. The youth group kept Bobby busy and happy. Mary and Kevin were always doing fun things in Sunday School. Bob and Betty really enjoyed being in the church choir.

Bob felt he could overlook the theological differences the big church had with Pleasant Street Church. They wouldn't matter when everything else felt so right, would they?

Still, both Bob and Betty grew increasingly uneasy with what they heard from the pulpit. And some of the Sunday School literature their kids brought home seemed at times at odds with ideas they had been taught when they were kids themselves.

Bob winced. *I wonder if we are doing our kids more harm than good?*

4

Who We Are

WHEN THE TELEPHONE rings at our house, we can look at the caller ID display before answering. The readout will reveal the listed name and number of the telephone from which the call originates.

Nevertheless, a name and number do not tell us everything about the person. He or she has a history and a particular situation in life that do not show up on the impersonal identification system.

A person's background can be painted in broad strokes, or it can be defined down to minute details. For example, if I'm traveling out of state, it is natural for people to ask where I'm from. When I say, "Missouri," that is probably enough information for the moment because it identifies me as *not* from where they are from. Yet, I am not just from a general place called Missouri. I live in a particular city. Within the city, I live in a particular part of town. And I live on an individual street. Furthermore, I live in a specific house.

The same basic principle works for family background. I have a particular European country from where my ancestors originally came. There is a specific locale where they first homesteaded in America. My history also includes a defined set of grandparents, parents, and my individual name. All of these historical points have had certain influences on me, while excluding other cultural experiences.

This will come as no surprise, but this process works the

same way for churches. The local church you attend has a historical denominational development that has shaped it in certain ways, including particular theological doctrines. Thus, we serve Christ through a variety of expressions of the Church. Jesus Christ is the Head of the Church, but the Body of Christ is quite diverse. When it comes to passing on our particular spiritual heritage, we need to know who we are as a part of the Christian family.

Who Are We?

Christians are not all alike. We are all believers in Christ, but we do not look alike, act alike, think alike. Or even believe all the same things. The Church is not generic Christianity, that is, a one-size-fits-all religion. There is wide diversity in the Church, yet we find a unity in Christ.

Paul explained it like this: "There are different kinds of gifts, but *the same Spirit*. There are different kinds of service, but *the same Lord*. There are different kinds of working, but *the same God* works all of them in all men" (1 Corinthians 12:4-6, emphases added).

If we are not all look-alike Christians, who are we? How does our denomination differ from other Christians? For us, "Wesleyan" and "Holiness" are the two most relevant aspects of our identity.

Our Theology Is Wesleyan

"Wesleyan" is the descriptive term that means our theology has been influenced by the thinking of John Wesley (1703-91). In addition, we sing a large number of hymns written by John's brother, Charles Wesley (1707-88).

John and Charles Wesley were raised in a pastor's home in England. They both studied at Oxford University. John was ordained in the Church of England in 1728. From 1735 until 1738 he was a missionary to the Native Americans in the colony of Georgia. Upon his return to England, Wesley's heart was "strangely warmed," his famous description of the moment he became certain that his sins were forgiven. From that point on, Wesley began to preach the necessity of a heartfelt faith. However, he met opposition within the Church of England, and one by one church pulpits were closed to him and his ideas.

Wesley's concentration was on "Christian perfection," a biblical term by which he meant holiness of heart and life. "Perfection" did not mean that a person could not be ignorant nor make a mistake. Rather, it meant that his or her heart was purified by faith in Christ. Love for God and neighbor filled the life of such a person.

In addition to his preaching about the experience of Christian perfection, Wesley approached theology in ways that still guide our theological reflections. Wesley believed that the Bible was the primary authority in matters of faith. However, he felt that the clearest understanding of Scripture occurs when we bring everything God has given us to bear on our study. Therefore, Wesley subjected every idea to four guidelines before he accepted it as a legitimate part of Christian belief. First, what did Scripture say about it? Did other scripture shed light on a particular passage? Second, what light did our God-given intellect shed on the subject? Next, how had the Church traditionally understood the matter? Finally, did the conclusion of our study match our experience? Over the years, this approach has kept Wesleyans from holding extreme and unsupportable theological positions.

The other theological gift Wesley handed down to us is his understanding, explanation, and emphasis on grace. Wesley believed in a sovereign God, but not in a predestining God. God is the Creator, Ruler, and Supreme Power of the universe, but He has not determined every detail that will happen in the future without regard to human decisions. God has given all human beings the ability to make choices, a freedom that is often used to make bad, even evil, decisions. Nevertheless, God never gives up on individuals. Rather, He draws them to himself by grace. No one living is beyond the reach of God's grace, if he or she will simply turn to Him and accept His gracious offer.

Wesley identified three types of grace that are in constant

operation in our world. First, there is *prevenient* grace. This is the grace that prepares a person before he or she becomes a Christian. It is revealed in the myriad, subtle ways that persons feel drawn to God. The second grace Wesley identified is *saving* grace. This is what accomplishes a person's salvation when he or she willingly turns to God. The third form, *sanctifying* grace, makes the believer holy and equips him or her for a lifetime of Christian growth and service.

Our Experience Is Holiness

Holiness churches share with other Evangelical churches the belief that Christians experience a personal, heartfelt conversion to Christ. The view that distinguishes us from other denominations is our belief in an experience after conversion called "entire sanctification." It is also referred to by other terms: "Christian perfection" (the term Wesley preferred because it is biblical), "perfect love," "heart purity," "the baptism of the Holy Spirit," and "Christian holiness."

For us, holiness means living a clean life wholly dedicated to God. A believer is entirely sanctified in an instant, but Christian maturity comes as the result of continual growth in grace. We live by Wesley's understanding that sin occurs when we decide to willingly transgress a law that God has made clear to humanity. This is in sharp contrast to those who believe Christians sin quite uncontrollably every day "in thought, word, and deed."

As a prominent Wesleyan scholar has stated: "It would be claiming too much to say that Christian perfection as delineated in the Scriptures and understood by Wesleyan theology has been taught and believed by the Church through the centuries. Actually, this teaching has often been condemned and maligned. Nevertheless, some form of [the] doctrine has been held in every age."[1]

Wesley was inspired by the writings of Irenaeus (A.D. 130—202) and Clement of Alexandria (ca. 150-ca. 215). When the monastic movement began around 270, it was because the monks wanted to dedicate their lives to Christian perfection.

Several of them wrote extensively on the subject, such as Macarius the Egyptian (304-90) and Gregory of Nyssa (330-95).

However, two influential theologians, Augustine (354—430) and Thomas Aquinas (1225-74) moved the Church away from Christian perfection as something attainable in this life. The main reason was their belief that original sin cannot be overcome by grace in this world. Two persons associated with the 16th-century Protestant Reformation, Martin Luther (1483—1546) and John Calvin (1509-64), were heavily influenced by Augustine's thought. Though the Reformers revived the scriptural doctrine of justification by faith, they neglected a healthy doctrine of holiness. "It was the Church's great loss that Luther and Calvin were unable to overcome their Augustinian pessimism concerning the possibilities of grace. By failing to develop a full-orbed teaching of sanctification, the Reformers left a spiritual vacuum in Protestantism."[2]

Groups that directly influenced John Wesley's spiritual formation filled that vacuum. These Christians were the German Pietists, the Quakers, and the Moravians. By the middle of the 18th century, Wesley had fully developed his thinking on the holy life. (His book, *A Plain Account of Christian Perfection*, was published in 1766.) Wesley's followers organized into "the people called Methodists" in England. In the late 18th century, as the American Revolution was unfolding, Wesley's vision of holiness spread to North America. The Methodist Church in America was born as a result of those who preached both conversion and sanctification.

By the mid-19th century, the experience of Christian perfection was carried in the hearts of persons like Phoebe Palmer (1839-1908). Since the beginning of the 20th century, Holiness folks have gathered in our own denominations, spreading the news of holiness across the world for the past 100 years. It is a distinct and heartfelt Christian message, handed down to us from John Wesley, who believed God raised him up and entrusted his people with this biblical doctrine. Some have even described the mission of Holiness churches as "Christianizing Christianity."

Passing On Our Faith

We do not apologize for being Wesleyan-Holiness Christians. The doctrine has possessed many of the greatest theologians of the Christian Church through the centuries. And it is how we feel we can best follow Christ.

In that, we are like any other family. All families have particular values they cherish and certain characteristics that they feel identify who they are. They spend time passing on to their children in a variety of ways what their family believes and how it is expected to act. This shapes how the children understand themselves and behave in the world around them. A strong sense of identity and firm belief in cherished values is an important heritage of any family.

For the same reason, we must never water down our heritage so that it looks like generic Christianity. We highly value our Wesleyan-Holiness tradition. Yet, this attitude in no way excludes us from fellowshipping with other Christian groups. Though our doctrine may be distinct, it does not exclude other Christians. We recognize the diversity of theology in the Body of Christ, but we also recognize that we speak with a unique theological "accent."

The Christianity we desire to live before the world and to pass on to the next generation is not generic. Rather, it is specifically Wesleyan-Holiness. The next generation should be able to say definitely, "We are Wesleyan-Holiness Christians." That is the legacy we want to pass on to them. What we believe, what we teach in our churches, and how we behave in our personal lives shape our children's understanding of themselves and their relationship to God.

The world and our children should know why we belong to this denomination. One reason is that through this denomination we heard the gospel and believed in Christ for salvation. Another reason is that we cherish the church's beliefs, with its emphasis on holiness, that give us clear directions for growth into mature Christians. And a reason we like to hang around Holiness folks is because we feel that the fellowship among these believers is a little touch of heaven on earth, a foretaste of what is to come.

In summary, we believe strongly in Wesleyan-Holiness churches because:

- They preach the saving and transforming gospel of Christ.
- They teach that we can live above sin in this life.
- They are optimistic about the power of God's grace to transform lives.
- They feel the whole world is truly "their parish"; anyone who chooses to receive Christ as Savior can join the kingdom of God.

That is who we are. Who could ask for more?

Notes:

1. William M. Greathouse, *From the Apostles to Wesley* (Kansas City: Beacon Hill Press of Kansas City, 1979), 32.

2. Ibid., 97.

Scripture: 1 Corinthians 12:4-6 (background on holiness: Romans 6:22; 2 Corinthians 7:1; Ephesians 4:22, 24; Hebrews 12:14)

A Glimpse of the Real World

"Whatcha working on there, Dad?" Bobby Christian leaned over his father's shoulder and peered at the words on the computer screen.

"A mission statement."

"A what?"

"A mission statement. Our church board asked me to work on this for our next meeting. It's a few sentences that explain the purpose of our church. We want to write them so we have a clear picture about what our church is supposed to do."

"That's easy. I can tell you in one sentence what the purpose of church is. It's to make you sit still while they bore you to death!"

Bob shook his head. "I don't think that's what Jesus had in mind for the Church. And the pastor would probably be disappointed to hear it. Besides, that wouldn't look very good on a promotional brochure, would it? The real purpose of the Church is . . ."

While he searched for the right words, Bob thought, *How can I explain the purpose of the Church to my son?*

5

Being the Church

CHURCH. It is one of those words that has so many meanings, we have to use it in a sentence in order to know what it means.

"Have you seen the new church they built down on Pleasant Street?" Obviously, the question concerns a building. A building unlike a library, a school, or a residence. A building in which people gather to hold worship services, Sunday School classes, and fellowship suppers.

"This church has been meeting here since 1945." Now we're talking about people. The people of a local congregation. The group of believers who worship together and know themselves to be the church.

"The Church is under attack by forces opposed to Christianity." This is referring to those who believe in Christ, no matter where they are located in the world. Usually we describe the worldwide Church with a capital C, indicating the universal, sometimes invisible collection of believers.

In this chapter, we move past understanding that the church is a building in which we Christians gather for various activities. Our focus is on the Church as the people of God.

The Church Is Alive

The Church is not merely an abstract idea. The Church is a living group of people. They come from all walks of life. Some are married; some are single. Some are old; many are young.

Some are healthy; others are ill. Many are happy; some are sad. They have all the characteristics of living human beings, and they believe in Jesus Christ as their Savior.

These living persons gather in local congregations all around the world every Sunday. It makes no difference whether they number 5 or 5,000; they do the same basic things. They sing. They pray. They listen to sermons. In short, they worship God in the name of their Lord and Savior Jesus Christ and go out to serve their neighbors in need.

The believers who constitute the Church are not only alive in human terms but also alive in the Spirit. It is the Spirit that makes the Church different from other groups of gathered human beings. Social clubs can meet and enjoy good times of fellowship. School groups can meet and conduct the business of educating our young. Yet, the Church is more than the human spirit of camaraderie of those groups because of the presence of the Holy Spirit within it.

At the "birthday" of the Church, which we know as Pentecost, the Holy Spirit descended upon the believers and empowered them for their mission to the world. That same Spirit today guides the Church as it continues Christ's work on earth.

The real foundation of the Church is Christ. The Church is called out of the world and established in the world by God through Christ. The goal of the Church is to become more like Christ in His mission and in His character. The Church is not a human achievement, nor is it simply gatherings of like-minded individuals who have formed support groups against the dangers of the world. God has called the Church together through Christ. Christ reveals God's agenda to the Church, gives its people a new identity and nature, and sends them out to continue His work in the world.

As a living organism made up of real persons, the Church encounters all the variety in life. It celebrates the joys of newborn believers. It buries its saints who have finished their course. It expands the family as new projects reach more and more people. It suffers the anxiety of growing pains and all sorts of other difficulties to which human life is prone. The Church exists in all kinds of sizes and states of health, but it is always alive.

The Church Is Active

The Church has a God-given mission. Jesus articulated it to the first disciples shortly before He ascended into heaven. He said, "Therefore go and make disciples of all nations, baptizing them in the name of the Father and of the Son and of the Holy Spirit, and teaching them to obey everything I have commanded you" (Matthew 28:19-20).

We refer to this as "the Great Commission." In it, we see a threefold task for the Church.

First, the Church is actively engaged in spreading the gospel of Jesus Christ worldwide. People become disciples of Jesus when they place their trust in Him. We refer to such disciples as Christians, that is, followers of Christ. They can only come to believe in Christ if they hear about Him. And they will not hear about Him unless someone preaches about Christ to them. That is the mission of the Church, to tell everyone about the saving power of Jesus Christ.

Second, the Church is to baptize believers into the fellowship of the Church. The Church is active in maintaining the sacraments, the holy rituals established and commanded by the Lord. Baptism is one such sacrament. The Lord's Supper is another. The Church preserves these traditions by actively engaging in the sacraments.

Third, the Church teaches how to live Christian lives. That means reminding its people of all the things Christ taught and encouraging them to live in ways Christ modeled.

The Church Is Where

The Church of Jesus Christ exists everywhere in the world. In some lands Christians are highly visible and maybe even taken for granted. In other areas of the world, the Church is invisible, hidden from cultures that despise the name of Christ.

Wherever the Church exists, there is a local expression of

it. A group of believers meet together somewhere—in a private house or a large cathedral, in an open park or a beautiful church building. When they meet as a local congregation, the work of the Church gets done. That is how we learn that the Church is where . . .

. . . sinners hear the good news of Jesus and receive salvation from their sins.

. . . disciples learn to grow in the grace and knowledge of the Lord Jesus Christ.

. . . Christians reach out to help other people with all kinds of physical, emotional, and spiritual needs.

So we can say that the Church, the living and active believers in Christ, gathers to worship and scatters to serve.

Saving the Church

God through Christ called the Church into existence. The Church has a God-given mission to evangelize the world through preaching, sacraments, teaching, and serving.

Unfortunately, not everyone has obeyed the call. In fact, it often looks as if interest in the Church is waning. Fewer people attend church each Sunday than used to be the case. Some congregations are barely hanging on to their existence. And in this age of entertainment and pleasure, there are many other attractions to entice our youth away from church.

Of course, this is nothing new. Even during the earliest days of the Church, a letter warned Christians about the need to persevere in the face of declining faith. "Let us not give up meeting together, as some are in the habit of doing, but let us encourage one another" (Hebrews 10:25).

All the same, giving up is a temptation sometimes. Church attendance is down. A wide variety of non-Christian spiritual beliefs are growing. More and more people ignore our attempts at evangelism. At times, even our own children appear uninterested in our faith.

Sometimes it seems as if no one wants to be a Christian anymore. So, what can we do? The Church has seen hard times before. Still, as we encourage each other and continue to faithfully meet together, the Church goes on, despite difficulty, apathy, or even persecution. And the Church needs to continue for two very important reasons.

First, *the church is our focal point for worship, teaching, and fellowship.* The Lone Ranger is not an apt symbol of Christianity. None of us goes it alone or accomplishes faith by individual effort, despite the loud message we hear from our culture that glorifies individuality.

Christian faith is a cooperative activity. We hear and respond to the gospel message in the context of other believers, and we live out the faith in the fellowship of believers. We are called out of a life of sin and called into the task of spreading the Good News.

As the gathered community, the church worships God. It takes a variety of spiritual gifts to offer proper adoration. It requires those who preach, those who sing, those who pray, and those who participate. Worship does not need a large number of persons, but it does require being together. As Jesus said, "For where two or three come together in my name, there am I with them" (Matthew 18:20).

As the gathered community, the church learns about God. Sunday School classes, small-group discussions, and sermons that explain the Scriptures all teach us how to be more like Christ. In this way, the church learns how to fulfill its mission to the world.

In the midst of gathering for worship and coming together for teaching, the church enjoys sweet fellowship. Friendships are bonded. Families grow. Strangers are welcomed. And thus the church practices for the great festival of rejoicing at the marriage supper of the Lamb (see Revelation 19:6-9).

Second, but just as important, *the Church is the context for passing the faith to the present and future generations.* The Church needs to survive in order to continue spreading the truth about God in a culture that hears so many false spiritual voices. The Church must keep on speaking for God and godly living in a society that has given itself over to the deafness of secularism. The Church has to persist in being light in the spiritual darkness and salt in the bland salad of cultural sameness.

It is imperative that the Church continue so that the next generation will be able to hear God's voice. If the Church disappears, who will speak for God? If the Church no longer exists, how will hungry hearts find true spiritual satisfaction?

If we do not pass on our faith to our children, the Church might die out in only one more generation. Yet, the good news is this: The Church will survive. It has survived hundreds of years of persecution. It has survived hundreds of years of apathy. It has weathered every storm this world has ever generated to try to bring it down. Yes, the Body of Believers will survive, for the Church has been called out and established by God through Christ. The Church is guaranteed and led by God through the Holy Spirit. Death and evil will never destroy it.

So we march into the unknown future, secure in the knowledge that we belong to God. We remain the Church— God's lighthouse in a sin-darkened world.

Scripture: Matthew 18:20; 28:19-20; Hebrews 10:25; Revelation 19:6-9

A Glimpse of the Real World

As the Christian family drove home from church, Mary was crying.

"What's wrong?" her mother asked.

"I don't like my Sunday School teacher anymore."

"Why not?"

"She taught us a memory verse today."

"You don't like to memorize Scripture?" Betty asked.

"That's not it. The memory verse was fine. It was 'Be kind and compassionate to one another, forgiving each other, just as in Christ God forgave you' (Ephesians 4:32)."

"So what's wrong then?"

"After we learned the verse, she yelled at Joey for interrupting class. He was just trying to tell her he was sad that his dog died, but she was mean to him and told him to sit still."

Betty took a deep breath. Before she could think of what to say to the crying girl, Kevin piped up. "Mommy, what's a hypocrite?"

Oh, no. Here we go, thought Betty.

6

Matching Words and Actions

HOW MANY times have you heard someone say, "Christians are hypocrites!"

That is easy to say, and it is widely believed.

What is a hypocrite anyway? It's really pretty simple. If we think someone's actions do not match their words, we label them a hypocrite. Often people have such high expectations of Christians, it takes very little to disappoint them. So they jump quickly to saying, "Christians are hypocrites!"

But is it true?

That's what we need to find out. If we are going to pass on the Christian faith to the next generation, it is important that our deeds match our words. So we need to understand what a hypocrite really is to make sure we can avoid being called one.

Hypocrisy Is a Mask

When someone fails to behave as we think he or she should, we often consider that hypocrisy. Yet, hypocrisy is not the same as simple failure. Hypocrisy involves intentional deceit. Hypocrites are persons who, on purpose, try to make people think they are something other than what they really are. Hypocrites are those who put on masks or facades in order to conceal how they really are inside.

On the other hand, what is often mistaken for hypocrisy is simply failure to live up to what we had hoped. For example, we may very well promise more than we can deliver, like when we say, "I'll always be there for you." When we find we are not able to "be there" at the depth someone needs, that does not make us a phony; it means we cannot perform at the level we wanted.

Sometimes non-Christians accuse Christians of hypocrisy (that is, intentional deceit) when what they are actually seeing are the human shortcomings of Christians. Non-Christians often place higher expectations on Christians than they do anyone else. In fact, they erroneously expect Christians to be perfect. No human being is perfect in the sense that he or she can never make a mistake. Christians remain imperfect in that human sense as long as they are alive.

Still, Christians must learn to deal with the high expectations others place on them. More importantly, Christians need to make sure that those closest to us—our children—do not mistakenly think that our Christian "walk" does not match our "talk."

We All Use Words

How do non-Christians expect us to talk?

Let's imagine we're taking a little survey. We're asking several people that question. Really, some of the answers, though negative, would not be surprising.

Topping everyone's list would be: *No lying.* This is no surprise. After all, not bearing false witness is one of the "Big Ten." No person of integrity should ever lie, Christian or not. However, there are lies and then there are lies. Where is the line drawn between bald-faced deception and shading the truth to be tactful? Between intentionally trying to deceive versus simply not hurting someone's feelings needlessly?

A close second on the non-Christian's expectation list is probably: *No swearing.* This may have lost its shock value, considering the language everyone hears on TV, the radio, and in the movies these days. People may have become so desensitized to cusswords that they wouldn't notice if one came out of a

Christian's mouth. On the other hand, Christians have found plenty of substitute swearwords—some obvious, some not—and maybe for many people this is a nonissue now. Should it be?

Running third would probably be: *No dirty jokes.* This one seems obvious, doesn't it? Yet it might not appear so evident to some Christians because the lines have been blurred. Though some Christians may be comfortable with jokes that are merely off-color, most non-Christians would be quick to label such a Christian joke-teller a hypocrite.

A fourth candidate would be: *No put-downs.* Non-Christians should not expect Christians to talk about other people the same way they do. A Christian should not be gossiping, ruining another's reputation, or directly calling another person hurtful names. If such language comes from a Christian, he or she should be prepared to wear the hypocrite label.

From that point on, our survey gets a little fuzzy. Certain individual non-Christians may hold opinions that the majority do not share. Yet, they use these ideas to judge Christians. For example, some people expect Christians to be open-minded about all religious ideas. When Christians state their convictions clearly, non-Christians accuse them of being judgmental. Furthermore, some non-Christians, believing that Christians should never be rude, mistake directness for rudeness. Others think Christians should never talk loudly or raise their voices in anger. Some even go so far as to expect Christians to never laugh, as if they have no sense of humor.

We can summarize how non-Christians expect Christians to talk in a positive way. Their expectation is that Christians will say kind things and will be understanding. Of course, in the extreme, "kind" could mean they expect nothing but sweetness and light and "understanding" could mean they expect Christians to tolerate everything.

With so much room for debate and misunderstanding, we should ask another question: What does the New Testament say to us about Christian conversation? Jesus mentioned it in His teaching. Paul and James wrote about it in their letters.

When Jesus delivered what we refer to as the Sermon on the Mount, He touched on the topic of swearing oaths. He did not mean cursewords. He meant the kind of oath that guarantees we will do something, as we used to say, "You have my word on it."

Jesus instructed His listeners not to try to guarantee their promises by anything other than their own word. Everything in heaven and on earth belongs to God. Therefore, they should not invoke anything above, below, or on the surface to back up their promise. Instead, Jesus said, "Simply let your 'Yes' be 'Yes,' and your 'No,' 'No'" (Matthew 5:37). Simply do what you say you will; nothing more, nothing less. As the later adage stated it, "Let your word be your bond."

The apostle Paul had more to say directly about conversation. He warned the Christians at Rome about those who would cause division by "smooth talk and flattery" (Romans 16:18). He was telling them to stay away from those tools of intentional deceit.

To the Christians at Ephesus, Paul wrote, "Do not let any unwholesome talk come out of your mouths, but only what is helpful for building others up" (Ephesians 4:29). Then he went on to list three other kinds of talk that should never be associated with Christians—"obscenity, foolish talk or coarse joking" (5:4).

Finally, in his Epistle to the Colossians, Paul gave a good summary of his teaching. He wrote a memorable sentence to guide Christians and their words. "Let your conversation be always full of grace, seasoned with salt" (4:6). James added the eternal perspective when he wrote, "Speak and act as those who are going to be judged by the law that gives freedom" (2:12).

Actions Speak Louder than Words

If what we do contradicts what we say, well, you know what they'll call us. So we have to ask ourselves: How does the world expect Christians to act?

Everyone expects Christians to be ones who do the right

thing. First and foremost, Christians are expected to be honest. Along with honesty comes the expectation of reliability. If you can't trust a Christian, who can you ever trust?

Not far behind, people expect Christians to love. Though some people may have sentimental ideas about love and be surprised when a Christian's actions do not match their view, love is, in fact, a defining characteristic of Christianity. Jesus told us to love God with everything we are and to love our neighbors as much as we love ourselves (Matthew 22:37-39). He also told us that no greater love can be shown than when a person loves another enough to die for him or her (John 15:13). Jesus exhibited supreme love when He died on Calvary for humanity's sins (1 John 3:16). And He expected love to be the clear sign of who His disciples are (John 13:35). Love is so important to Christianity that Paul said, "The only thing that counts is faith expressing itself through love" (Galatians 5:6).

However, if Christians are anything, they are misunderstood. Paul had to warn the Colossians, "Be wise in the way you act toward outsiders" (4:5). It is not uncommon for non-Christians to take honesty, reliability, and loving-kindness as characteristics of weakness. Then they think that Christians are pushovers, easy and gullible targets. Some might even use the word "wimpy" to describe their idea of a typical Christian.

That brings us to another interesting question.

Was Jesus a Wimp?

The image of a meek and mild Jesus is a popular one. Often He is portrayed as speaking and acting very gently and quietly. We often think of Him humbly allowing all the events surrounding His arrest and death simply to happen. Do those ideas mean Jesus was a wimp?

No. Jesus was no spineless, wishy-washy person who made sure He always went along with the program so as not to make waves. Rather, Jesus was honest, compassionate, and forthright against anything that was wrong.

Jesus told the truth, even when it meant stirring up a scene.

In the Gospels, the word "hypocrites" comes from Jesus' mouth 15 times. He knew the truth about the deceptive practices of the religious leaders. Each time He used the word, He confronted another aspect of their hypocrisy. And the religious leaders knew He spoke the truth.

When Jesus came to the Temple and saw the great amount of unscrupulous business being conducted there, He did not slink away, saying, "Oh, well. There's nothing that can be done about it." Rather, He acted. "Jesus entered the temple area and began driving out those who were buying and selling there. He overturned the tables of the money changers and the benches of those selling doves, and would not allow anyone to carry merchandise through the temple courts" (Mark 11:15-16).

However, Jesus was not harsh with those who were not hypocrites. He felt for those in need. "When he saw the crowds, he had compassion on them, because they were harassed and helpless, like sheep without a shepherd" (Matthew 9:36). When His friend Lazarus died, Jesus "was deeply moved in spirit and troubled" (John 11:33). He did not cry out of weakness. Rather, He shed tears of understanding and sorrow.

A Legacy of Trust

If Christians are to be like Jesus, then we must also be honest, compassionate, and willing to confront wrong where we find it. In doing so, we will have integrity, that is, our walk will match our talk.

If people—especially our children—see that our actions match our words, they will want to know more about Christ. They will want to learn more about the One who causes us to live lives of integrity and wholeness.

It happened in the Early Church. The first Christians not only claimed to be followers of Christ (at the risk of death, we must remember!) but also lived Christian lives. In addition to fulfilling their jobs as working-class citizens, "they devoted themselves to the apostles' teaching and to the fellowship, to the breaking of bread and to prayer" (Acts 2:42). The reaction of the public is summed up in one phrase, "Everyone was filled with awe" (v. 43). And the result was new converts—daily (v. 47).

Before we relax and say, "Well, they can just watch my life, and they'll know I'm a Christian," there is something we must remember. The public proclamation of the gospel is central. There is certainly a place for "lifestyle evangelism" in our world. Yet, it is highly unlikely that anyone would have been converted on the Day of Pentecost had not Peter, or someone like him, stood up and spoken up. The Word must be lived, but also it must be proclaimed.

Jesus said that when the Holy Spirit comes, "he will convict the world of guilt in regard to sin" (John 16:8). To use a courtroom analogy, Christians are not called to be lawyers, judges, or juries to convince sinners that they are guilty or assign them a penalty for their iniquity. Rather, Christians are called to be witnesses, sharing the good news that there is a Savior, living consistent lives before the world, and relaxing in the assurance that we are working hand in hand with the Holy Spirit. We are to proclaim; He will convict. That takes a great burden off our shoulders.

Someone might say, "Aren't things tougher now than in the first century?" They are certainly different and much more complex. And there are a growing number of people in our day who do not have even the slightest residue of religious training. That means we must do a better job of teaching what the Bible says, and answering their questions when we get the chance. And that points up the importance of Bible training, such as we do in Sunday School and small groups, both as an outreach tool for the church and as a means of teaching people about the Lord.

At the same time, it is important that our behavior match our words in our own homes. Our children watch our actions, and they are sharp at noticing if an inconsistency occurs between what we say and what we do. If we claim to be Christians and yet do unchristian things, what will our children learn? Will they grow up thinking it's OK for Christians to tell "little white lies"? Or that it's acceptable for Christians to be honest most of the time rather than all the time? Or that going to church on Sunday is top priority unless . . .

Well, you get the picture. There may be a thousand behaviors that we could talk about here. Still, the important point is that children whose lives we want to influence for the Lord live right in our homes with us. They need to clearly understand the difference between human failure and hypocrisy. We may fall short of the goals we set because we have limited resources, but we should never intentionally deceive anyone into thinking we are something we are not.

The faith we want to pass on is a sincere one that we live consistently before our children every day.

Just like believers in the first century, we, too, must live consistent Christian lives and proclaim the gospel in such a way as to cause our children, our friends, and our acquaintances to ask, "What must I do to be saved?" (Acts 16:30). If our actions match our words, if our good character is seen in our good deeds, then people will know we have integrity. If we speak and live consistently, they can be sure that in the Christian life, "what you see is what you get"—in every time and every place.

And maybe then people will stop hanging the "hypocrite" label on us.

Scripture: Matthew 5:37; 9:36; 22:37-39; Mark 11:15-16; John 11:33; 13:35; 15:13; 16:8; Acts 2:42-43, 47; 16:30; Romans 16:18; Galatians 5:6; Ephesians 4:29, 32; 5:4; Colossians 4:5-6; James 2:12; 1 John 3:16

A Glimpse of the Real World

The Christian household was chaotic.

Bob had rushed in the door, bearing sacks of fast food for supper. Betty had worked late because a meeting at the office had run overtime. Bobby barely finished his homework, and Mary was late getting home from soccer practice.

Only Kevin seemed to be at ease, peacefully munching on potato chips as he watched the last few minutes of his favorite TV show.

"We have to hurry," Betty shouted from the bedroom. "We have to be at church in 15 minutes for the revival service."

A chorus of groans echoed back to her from her three children.

"Why do we have to go to revival? It's so boring!" Kevin whined.

"I wish I went to Suzie's church," chimed in Mary. "They don't have revivals."

"Yeah. No one needs revivals anymore. They're lame!" Bobby added.

"But we're going all the same," Bob stated. Still, he thought to himself, *Why do we put so much emphasis on revival and renewal anyway?*

7

Revival or Survival?

H AVE YOU EVER rooted around in an attic or the basement of a house where someone has lived a long time? It is not unusual to find old items in corners or behind other things. Objects that were once useful and meaningful now are dusty and unused. Simply looking at some of those old things can bring back pleasant memories of days long gone.

Buried in the dusty corners of some churches is an old word. It is a word that once was useful and meaningful. Lots of people have good memories of the word. Now it needs the dust blown off and looked over in a new light.

The word is "revival."

Revival is definitely an old word to those who have been around the church most of their lives. Many associate the word with a series of meetings (a week or longer) with a guest evangelist. For some church members, the length, the frequency, and even the "old-fashionedness" of such meetings have overshadowed their purpose.

Revival means renewal. A revival is a time for breathing new life into a religion that has lost its zeal. A revival is a time for individuals to be refreshed by the Holy Spirit and to renew their commitment to Christ. Revival is (literally) coming back to life, renewed and refreshed for the journey.

Why is "Revive Us Again" such a popular song among Evangelicals? Because we know that without periodic refreshing, our love can grow cold.

It is true on the human level. Unless we take time to re-fresh our acquaintances by spending time together or talking with each other, any friendship will fade away. In a marriage, without thoughtful deeds, loving comments, and weekends away, even the most committed love will lose its luster.

It is just as true on the spiritual level. We cannot expect to tell God we love Him once, never cultivate our relationship with Him, and then expect our Christian life to be vibrant and vital. We must consistently have times of refreshing and renewal of our faith in order to survive the long journey through life.

Christian renewal has both a group aspect and an individual component. Without renewal, a group of Christians can become dull in their faith, or worse, die off completely. They may keep up appearances, even have "a form of godliness" (2 Timothy 3:5), but they will really be "whitewashed tombs" (Matthew 23:27), beautiful on the outside but dead inside.

The warmth of a fire is the result of individual embers clustered together, combining their heat. An ember separated from the group will soon burn out. An ember that brings no personal warmth to the group will not add to the heat and will even contribute to the fire going out sooner. Add an *m*, and the same principle works for *members* as *embers*.

Revivals Have a Purpose

When a church holds a revival, a special time is set and a special effort is put forth. The time for the meetings is scheduled on the calendar. An evangelist is slated. Special music is planned. And then the whole enterprise is bathed in prayer, often for many weeks in advance.

Why go to all that trouble? Can't people feel refreshed in the regular church services? Why have a special emphasis?

Yes, people can and do find times of renewal in regular worship services. This is something that happens nearly every week for many who spend their weeks in secular, high-pressure jobs. However, intentionally setting aside time for refreshing often accomplishes more than the week-to-week activities.

Revival services have two specific purposes. Setting aside special time to concentrate on them is often necessary to accomplishing them.

First, the purpose of revival services is *to convert sinners*. Of course, that is an ongoing commitment in any Evangelical congregation. However, the special emphasis of a revival can sometimes get the attention of sinners that regular worship services do not. The appeal of the special music may attract them. They might suddenly understand the gospel message when the guest evangelist speaks, where they have tuned out the pastor saying the same things. It give members another opportunity to invite their friends simply because the meetings are out of the ordinary.

Second, the purpose of revival is *to renew Christians in their faith*. Some of the same dynamics of the revival that work on sinners accomplish times of refreshment for Christians. Often the music is inspiring to weary souls. Sometimes the evangelist's messages give new insights into the pastor's regular sermons. And seeing friends come to Christ can rejuvenate a person's own resolve to live for Christ.

Revival meetings are times for the Christian community to set aside their day-to-day business and concentrate as a group on being refreshed and renewed by the Holy Spirit. Evangelical churches continue the tradition of having revival meetings because they move everyone closer to the Lord.

We Also Need Personal Renewal

No one can rely on public revivals, which usually occur twice a year at most, as his or her sole means of spiritual growth. Each Christian must experience for himself or herself private times of renewal.

One way that happens is when Christians participate regularly in public worship services. What we refer to as "the means of grace" are available there. Hymns are sung. Scripture is read. Prayers are offered. Sermons are delivered. And sacraments are observed. God can and does speak to individuals through any and all of these means.

Another way Christians experience private times of renewal is through personal devotions. Many aids to private devotions are available. It all boils down to having a personal time of reading the Bible and praying. The ideal is to do this daily.

One result of consistent personal devotions is personal spiritual growth. Reading the Bible daily increases our knowledge and understanding of Scripture. The benefits of daily prayer almost go without saying. We gain so much when we talk to God about our concerns and listen to Him for guidance.

We realize another profit from personal times of refreshing. We bring insights to our group experiences that enrich the community of faith. What we learn in private, we can share in public. (We used to call this "testimony time.") Not only are we reminded of the feelings we had the first time we received the insight from the Lord, but also others benefit from our sharing with them.

We Have a Spiritual Heritage

Over the years, Christians have developed various ways of spending time with the Lord. These methods have become tried-and-true traditions for many Christians. They provide structure for perseverance in life and growth in grace.

Let's take a brief look at some of these traditional disciplines as ways to improve our devotional lives. First, the disciplines that have an interior focus; then, the ones that have an outward component; and finally, the communal practices of discipline.

Inner Disciplines:

- *Meditation* This is not meditation as it is popularly portrayed in Eastern religions. Rather, this means spending time thinking about the meaning of Scripture or contemplating the goodness of God. It is spending quiet time, considering spiritual things.
- *Prayer* Like a precious gold coin, prayer has two sides. Both are important, though one side often gets cut short in Evangelical circles. One part of prayer is talking to God. It is bringing our adoration, confes-

sion, thanksgiving, and supplications to the Lord. The other side of the coin is listening to God. We need to wait in silence to hear what God has to say to us in our spirits.

- *Fasting* Perhaps this is a discipline that we don't hear too much about anymore. However, fasting is an important part of spiritual practice. There are many different kinds of fasting besides not eating. Some may suit individual circumstances better than going without food.

- *Study* This is an important activity that goes beyond simply reading the biblical texts. It involves reading good books that explain the texts, as well as Christian books that will help us to grow in grace and knowledge.

Outward Disciplines:

- *Simplicity* This is the remedy for lives that are too full of things and too complicated by situations. The goal of this habit is to learn to live with "just enough" rather than to keep trying to amass more and more.

- *Solitude* Effective personal growth comes from spending time alone with God. The individual inner disciplines listed above can best be practiced without the distraction of having other people around.

- *Submission* This is giving up trying to control every detail of life (a futile endeavor anyway) and learning to accept life as it comes to us in the rhythms of grace. Practicing this discipline has a beneficial effect on those around us as well.

- *Service* This is making a habit of discovering what needs others have and finding ways to fulfill those requirements. This is where Christian love is put into visible action.

Corporate Disciplines:

- *Confession* This need not turn into a belief in a "sinning religion." We believe that sanctified Christians can and do live above sin in this life. However, sanctification has to do with heart purity, not immunity from human error. Therefore, as humans, we make mistakes and have shortcomings, which we can bring to God and others in the form of confession and be helped to overcome them.

- *Worship* It hardly seems necessary to remind Christians that we are to worship God. However, even regular attendance at worship services must be an intentional habit we develop, or we will miss out on what we refer to as "the means of grace."
- *Guidance* This discipline involves both giving and receiving spiritual guidance. It is intentionally aligning with a Christian friend with whom to share the journey of faith.
- *Celebration* This is an important attitude to have all the time. "Celebration is central to all the spiritual disciplines. Without a joyful spirit of festivity the disciplines become dull, death-breathing tools in the hands of modern Pharisees. Every discipline should be characterized by carefree gaiety and a sense of thanksgiving."*

Renewed for Life

We can't pass on a vital Christian faith if we allow it to grow stale through neglect. We must constantly renew our relationship with God to keep it fresh and pertinent, available for today's challenges. We find refreshing from the Lord in lots of ways. Special evangelistic meetings. Regular shared worship experiences. Daily personal devotions. Traditional spiritual disciplines. All these are paths to revival, not simply survival.

If we learn to develop the habits that help us continue to grow spiritually, we will see revival now and in the future. And so will our children.

Notes:

*Richard J. Foster, *Celebration of Discipline* (San Francisco: Harper, 1988), 191.

Scripture: Matthew 23:27; 2 Timothy 3:5

A Glimpse of the Real World

Bob Christian pushed his chair back from the table and sighed contentedly. "Now that was a good meal if I've ever had one."

"Yes, it was," his wife, Betty, agreed. "Even if it was Chinese takeout. Still, we ate it together as a family at our own table on our own plates."

"May I be excused?" Bobby asked.

"Not so fast, young man," his father said. "We haven't had family devotions yet. Kevin, go get my Bible off my nightstand, please."

"Mary, help me put these dirty dishes in the dishwasher," added Betty.

Kevin raced off to retrieve his father's Bible. Mary helped her mother. Bobby sat glumly at the table, slumping his shoulders and trying to wish himself somewhere else.

"What's the matter, Son?" Bob asked.

"When I go to Billy's house, they never read the Bible and pray after dinner. Why do we have to?"

Bob thought of lots of reasons, but he didn't say anything. In his tiredness, Bob wondered, *Are family devotions worth all the fuss?*

8

Faith Begins at Home

EVERY MORNING after breakfast, my father read a psalm and commented on its meaning. Then he read a portion of the New Testament, also along with commentary. Next, we all knelt around the living room furniture while my father prayed a long prayer that mentioned every missionary in the known world. We closed the prayer time with a unison recitation of the Lord's Prayer.

That was how we started every day. Of course, Eisenhower was in the White House, and we were barely halfway through the 20th century. Obviously, things have changed now that we're many years later into the first quarter of the 21st century.

I'd wager a dollar to a doughnut we'd be hard-pressed to find many families that begin their day like that now. How many families even eat breakfast together? It's more common, with our busy lifestyles, for each family member to grab something on the go as we scatter in separate directions. In fact, there is a multitude of handheld breakfast products made to accommodate just such a practice.

Were the "good old days" of my childhood better? In some ways, yes; in others, no. Are today's hurried-up lives better? For a generation now, people have debated whether the rising number of working parents (generally in two-parent families) is good or bad for the children. Some think the children suffer from hectic schedules and lack of parental attention. Others feel the children gain from better economic conditions.

How much time are we spending with our children? One researcher said, "A recent study showed parents in 1965 spent an average of 30 hours per week in direct contact with their children, while parents in 1985 spent only 17 hours each week. Other research indicates families today spend much more time watching television."[1] A 1998 Canadian study showed about 16 hours per week is still the average for parent-child interaction.[2]

What do the studies show that parents are doing during those hours with the children? The time includes "primary child care (bathing, dressing, teaching, supervising, counseling, driving, and feeding children), but also secondary child care (time spent with children doing other things, such as cooking, housework, hobbies, etc.) and shared leisure, . . . what many parents call 'quality' time—playing together, watching TV, or eating meals together."[3]

Numerous studies have shown that the nature of the time spent together is an important aspect for both parents and children. One researcher went on record to talk about the importance of quality time to a child's future. "Every minute that a parent spends one-on-one with each child . . . is like money in the bank in terms of reinforcing their relationship. I think it can certainly decrease the possibility or the probability of the children being involved in gangs, drug abuse, to other undesirable behaviors as they get older."[4]

The most pessimistic view says that the average father spends less than seven minutes a week in individual quality time with his children. An even more disturbing fact was discovered in a recent study. College-educated fathers spend less time with their children; and for every $10,000 more in income they earn, they spend five minutes less with their children on weekdays.[5] If we are only spending seven minutes a week, we can't afford to drop another five minutes just to make a few more dollars.

Whether we are spending several hours or seven minutes a

day with our children, we need to ask ourselves an important question. As our lives have become busier, have we found ways to continue to teach our children about our faith, not only for the sake of our Christian heritage but also to fulfill the biblical mandate?

Hear, O Israel

Things had changed for Israel by the time Moses gave his advice that is recorded in Deuteronomy 6. Forty years earlier, Moses and the people called Hebrews had left Egypt under rather unusual conditions. Since then they had experienced the demands of desert living, the horrors of war, and the temptation to follow other gods.

Since then they had become a nation.

Since then all the adults who left the land of the Nile had died, except three men—Moses, Caleb, and Joshua. Before long the trio would be a duet; only Caleb and Joshua would enter the Promised Land. God would lay Moses to rest in an unmarked grave.

First, however, Moses had some important words to speak. None are more significant than these: "Hear, O Israel: The LORD our God, the LORD is one" (v. 4). This English phrase, "the LORD our God, the LORD is one," is just four words long in the Hebrew. "Yahweh, our God, Yahweh, One" is the most literal translation.

Yahweh (YAH-way), usually translated "LORD" in modern versions, is not one of a group of gods who has a right to ask for Israel's attention and loyalty. Yahweh alone is to be worshiped. It is not that all other gods are secondary; there are no other gods.

Yahweh alone is God. These four words are the rock on which both Judaism and Christianity are built. Whatever else the Hebrews might have been tempted to believe was false unless it was in line with these four words.

Next come some of the most daring words of the Bible. "Love the LORD your God with all your heart and with all your soul and with all your strength" (v. 5). These words are a command, not a suggestion.

The command to love sounds a lot like the preacher who said to his congregation, "Love your neighbor—and that's an order!" How can we combine love with duty?

Herein lies the daring language of devotion. In that day few people, if any, worshiped their god because they loved him. They gave expensive sacrifices out of terror. The people of Israel were to obey the Lord out of love, not fear.

A duty to love. What an exciting idea! Obedience is transformed. No longer is it the slave's response to a master's whip. Suddenly, it has become the gentle reply to a God whose love is so great it took Him one day to a skull-shaped hill outside Jerusalem.

A love response of this intensity has great rewards. Moses passed on this mandate from God so that the Israelites, their children, and their children's children would fear the Lord and "enjoy long life" (v. 2). We would be well advised also to follow Moses' teaching in this regard.

The commandments spelled out in verses 4-5 "are to be upon your hearts" (v. 6). Verses 7-9 explain what to do with what is "upon your hearts." These verses list four specific ways to pass on this devotional love to the next generation.

- "Impress them on your children."
- "Talk about them" at home and away, at work and at play.
- "Tie them as symbols" on hands and foreheads.
- "Write them" on doors and gates, everywhere people enter or leave.

In essence, the most important quality of "quality time" spent with children is how we allow the love of God to permeate everything we do. This does not mean that every activity is overtly Christian, but it does mean that our love for Christ is the motivation behind everything we do. If Christ is the center of our lives, then that will be reflected in every activity of our lives—whether serious or fun. If we go about loving God completely, then everywhere our children turn they will find verbal or symbolic reminders of God's love for them and their love for God.

In the command to love Him totally, God gave the Israelites something important to pass on to the following generations. When Jesus reiterated this same command, He gave Christians the same important focus to pass on to future generations. All three Synoptic Gospels reported those words because they are so important (see Matthew 22:37-40; Mark 12:30-31; Luke 10:27).

How can we accomplish such devotion in our time-pressured lives?

Be Creative

Along with the increased complexity of our technological age have come increasingly creative ways to do what we need to do. The Hebrews of Moses and Jesus' times were probably limited to recitation of the Torah and talking about what the rabbis taught. Today, we have colorful children's books, videos, computers, CDs, and DVDs, just to name a few of the technologies available. By the time you read this, there will probably be a couple more that I haven't even heard of yet.

So the answer in our hurry-up world is to find creative ways to "impress" spiritual things on our children and "talk about them" as we live together day by day. The discussion that follows of a few ideas is not exhaustive. It is only meant to give some ideas how to get family devotions started again.

Given the probable low numbers of families that actually practice family devotions, old would be new for many. By old, I mean the scenario I described at the beginning of this chapter. The family gathers, a parent reads and comments on a portion of Scripture, and everyone who wants takes a turn at praying. Then the devotional time ends with a unison recitation of the Lord's Prayer or the Apostles' Creed.

If gathering the family around the Bible every morning is not a workable option, there are still other alternatives for families. Here are a few ideas:

- Get the Bible and devotional books on cassette tape or CD, and listen to them as you travel from one activity to

another. This can be enjoyable for all ages and is a good
alternative to the "noise" of commercial radio.

- Choose a Bible story video to watch together. Anyone
  with small children knows how they latch onto favorite
  videos and play them over and over. A good Bible story
  video is a far better choice than most of the secular children's fare available.
- With older children, watch a good video together and
  discuss the theological themes. Not only will this reinforce what we believe as Christians, but also it will help
  the children become skilled at recognizing where cultural
  beliefs contrast with Christian beliefs.
- Make 52 Scripture memory cards, putting one memorable
  verse on each card for each week of the year. Then say
  the memory verse to each other as you pass in the house.
  Or, since the number of cell phones has increased, review
  the verse as you talk on the phone with each other.
- Here's a difficult one: Turn off the TV and shut off the
  radio—even for one evening. Spend the time as a family,
  reading or listening to Christian music or a Christian
  book on tape or CD. You might even prepare an object
  lesson to teach the children one concept of the Christian
  faith in a PowerPoint program.
- Here's another hard one: Cancel one nonfamily activity
  (such as a round of golf or a shopping trip), stay at home,
  and spend the time talking with your spouse and children
  about spiritual things.

One writer/father explained how he and his wife helped
their children feel loved and appreciate family time together. He
called it "taking out *love insurance*." Here's how this "policy"
works:

> After the children's toys have been picked up, home-
> work has been completed, and pajamas are on, we take a
> few minutes for a special quiet time. We gather the family
> together and read a favorite Bible story, sing a song, chant a
> nursery rhyme, or play a short game. We then visit with

each child—individually—for a few minutes. . . . My wife and I listen attentively as the children talk about the events of their days.[6]

When it comes to having daily family devotions, there are many ways to go about it. Don't hesitate to try new things, to find the ways that work best for your family situation. Be creative and just do it!

Be Intentional

Some would say that conversation at the family dinner table has disappeared forever. It's not so much that people don't talk while eating; it's that hardly any family sits down to a meal together anymore. Fast food and full schedules have severely hampered that activity.

Others would be quick to say that is not necessarily true. Families still eat together and talk to each other.

The truth probably resides somewhere between those two positions. Each family must look at its own situation and determine to make any adjustments that might be necessary. In many families, for dinner conversation to survive, family dinnertime must be revived. It will not happen accidentally; we must be intentional about re-creating it.

Here are some ideas that might help:

- Even if the fare is fast food, make a point of eating it at the table together. And talk to each other. Don't let the old adage "Don't talk with your mouth full" stop you. Take turns talking while the rest chew.

- Make a new rule: Every evening the family will eat together around the table, no matter what the menu. This will require some scheduling changes (and enduring some complaints), but most of them can be worked out. Meetings and ball games can still be attended *after* supper together. It will be worth the effort.

- If you can't work out an every-night schedule, consistently plan one night a week when no other activity will be scheduled except dinner and conversation. Then review the news of the day or week and discuss whatever theological significance it has.

One small town decided to carry the idea of a family night into the whole community. They planned for one night on which nothing was scheduled. No homework. No soccer. No meetings of any kind, including church meetings. "It took a committee of 18 people seven months and six meetings to plan, but Ridgewood [New Jersey] . . . is finally taking what heretofore only a blizzard could impose: a night off."[7] If a whole town can coordinate even one family night a year, surely individual families could manage it once a week.

Are Devotions Important?

Daily family devotions. Family dinner conversations. Are they really that important?

The answer is "yes" for a couple of good reasons. First, studies show that family is still a major influence on children and teens. That is why we see commercials calling conversation between parents and their children the "antidrug." Second, family devotions and dinner conversations are time-honored and time-tested methods for instructing the children. They are opportunities to reinforce our faith in God and teach our children to "love the LORD your God with all your heart and with all your soul and with all your strength" (Deuteronomy 6:5).

Are these things gone forever? They don't have to be—if we are creative and intentional about passing on the faith.

Notes:

1. Robert DelCampo, quoted in "Giving the Gift of Quality Time to Children," New Mexico State University College of Agriculture and Home Economics news release (December 1, 1995), <www.cahe.nmsu.edu/news>.

2. Robert Glossop, "Who Has Time for Children?" The Vanier Institute of the Family news release (November 20, 2000), <www.vifamily.ca>.

3. "Parents Put In a Full Day's Work Raising Two Children," Cornell University news release (May 8, 1997), <www.news.cornell.edu>.

4. DelCampo, "Quality Time."

5. "The More Money You Make, the More Time You Take from Your Children," *Family and Home* (July 2000), <www.laurushealth.com>.

6. Rich Gorton, "Love Insurance," *Outlook* (April 14, 2002), 9.

7. "Are They Relaxed Yet?" *USA Today* (March 26, 2002), <www.usatoday.com>.

Scripture: Deuteronomy 6:1-9; Matthew 22:37-40; Mark 12:30-31; Luke 10:27

A Glimpse of the Real World

Kevin had a quizzical look on his face. He held a brochure from Pleasant Street Church in his hand.

"Mom?"

"Yes, Son," Betty replied, looking up from her crossword puzzle. "What is it?"

"What does this mean?" Kevin read the words on the brochure to his mother. "Our church can be your family."

"Well, you know, it means the church can be like a family."

"I thought you had to be related to each other to be a family. Like our family is you and me, and Mary, and Bobby, and Dad. We all live together 'cause we're a family."

"Well, yes. That is one kind of family."

"Are there other kinds?"

"What about Jenny and her mom? Jenny doesn't have any brothers or sisters, and her dad doesn't live with them. Are they a family?"

"I guess so. They're related."

"OK. What about Mr. Hill next door? Is he a family?"

Kevin thought a moment. "No, he lives by himself. He's not a family."

"I see. Don't you think he needs a family? And maybe Jenny and her mom need other people too?"

"Yeah, I guess so."

"So families come in all kinds of patterns, and they are all welcome at church."

Kevin smiled. "Oh, I get it."

I hope you do, Betty thought. *I want my children to understand that their church is just like an extended family that cares for them and loves them.*

9

Family Is a Verb

A MINISTER WAS greeting a new family at the door of the church. After meeting Mom and Dad, the pastor was introduced to three-year-old Andy. The minister asked him about the baby in the blanket-covered carrier. "Is this little angel a member of your family?"

Andy answered, "No, she's just my sister."

Apparently Andy couldn't define "family." If pressed, could we do any better?

Family is an important concept, but one that is undergoing a rapid change. What do we mean when we say ours is a "family church"? How do we relate to each other as family these days? Does the word "family" only apply to those who live under the same roof, or can the concept extend to persons who act like family to us?

In this chapter we want to explore what family is, because nurture is an important idea. We need to remember that children and adults need the relationships of family—both their relatives and the church—to help them hear and respond to the voice of God.

Defining Family

Probably the most typical idea that comes to mind when someone asks, "What is a family?" are the people who were portrayed in the TV series *Father Knows Best*. For most people, the Andersons were an ideal family. The father went to work every day at the office. The mother stayed home and efficiently ran the household. They had two children, one of each gender. The four of them lived in the same suburban house, and each had a clearly defined role in the family.

Oh, if things were only that simple!

The Andersons may have been perceived as the typical family in 1950s America, but things have changed since then. A comparison of the 2000 U.S. Census with the 1950 one shows that the number of reported families practically doubled (an 88 percent increase) while the number of married couples only grew by 50 percent. Also, in 1950 married couples accounted for 47.2 percent of the total population, while by 2000 their number had dropped to 38.7 percent.*

Bottom line: less marriage, more redefinition of "family."

In today's culture, the definition of family is hard to pin down. The variations can seem almost endless. We can find families that have children but one of the parents is absent, through death, divorce, or abandonment. Some families have one or more grandparents living with them, or maybe both parents are absent and the grandparents are taking over the parenting roles. Perhaps the mother and father are not married but have children, or a couple without children live together. And there is increasing incidence of families being headed by two "moms" or two "dads" as gay persons try to reconfigure the concept.

Even some biblical examples do not fit our modern ideas of family. For example, look at 1 Samuel 1:1-2. There we see that Elkanah (el-KAN-uh) was the head of a family that included two wives; one had children, the other did not. This is quite removed from our idea of one father, one mother, and two children. Yet, this was the family into which Samuel was eventually born.

Perhaps "family" is more of a verb than a noun. Without depreciating the place of the traditional family, it would seem that the *function* of family might be as important as the *composition* of the family. A variety of different configurations can operate to nurture the people in the group. Even close friends can behave like family for each other. Certainly, the church should be a nurturing extended family.

Does that mean that the Christian definition of family must accept all variations that society presents us? No, there are moral boundaries. Certain groupings of individuals in families are incompatible with our ability to live holy lives. Immoral behaviors do not lead to lives of holiness.

However, in drawing the lines of distinction, do we inadvertently exclude some persons who are not immoral? What about single-parent families? Or a family consisting of only a single person, whether formerly married or never married? How do we view childless couples, whether it is their choice or not? Do we define "family" so narrowly that we exclude these varieties?

To try to answer that, let's look at Samuel's story and consider what the purpose of family is.

Samuel's Story

Those of us who watch television, and that's most of us, are used to being teased. One of the dictionary definitions of the word "tease" is "to persuade by persistent small efforts."

That's how television treats us. The program starts with 45 seconds of action or humor designed to capture our attention and keep us tuned in. Then, we are entertained by a few minutes of sometimes interesting, but often offensive, commercials. Finally, the program itself begins. It moves quickly—the images changing every seven to nine seconds.

The quickest way to kill interest would be to say, "There was a certain man from Ramathaim, a Zuphite from the hill country of Ephraim, whose name was Elkanah son of Jeroham, the son of Elihu, the son of Tohu, the son of Zuph, an Ephraimite" (1 Samuel 1:1).

Before the announcer got to the word "Elkanah," we would have said, "Honey, can't you find anything better on TV?"

In the days when storytelling was an art as well as the only way a nation remembered its history, that's the way stories began. In hearing about Elkanah, we've just heard the beginning of one of the significant stories in the Old Testament. In this narrative we hear about a mother's dream, a nation's despair, and a boy's destiny.

Babies Are on Everyone's Mind

While some women carry placards declaring a woman's right to abort her unborn child, other women buy expensive drugs hoping to get pregnant. Helping people make babies is big business these days. That makes the story of Hannah a familiar one. We can identify with the emotions of the story, even though it took place more than 3,000 years ago.

It's a simple story. A man named Elkanah had two wives, relatively common back then. One of them had several children, the other none. The one who had no children, Hannah, was his favorite wife.

The annual trip to worship at Shiloh was not a happy time for Hannah. Peninnah (peh-NIN-ah), the other wife, provoked her to deep sorrow. Not even Elkanah's gentle care could relieve the sadness.

One night, after the evening meal, Hannah took her burden to the Lord. She stood outside the sanctuary, for that was as close to the Lord's house as a woman was allowed to get. Her despair was so great she moved her lips in prayer but no sound escaped.

"Eli [the priest] thought she was drunk and said to her, 'How long will you keep on getting drunk? Get rid of your wine'" (1:13-14).

"'Not so, my lord,' Hannah replied, '. . . I have been praying here out of my great anguish and grief'" (vv. 15-16).

"Eli answered, 'Go in peace, and may the God of Israel grant you what you have asked of him'" (v. 17).

So she did.

And God did.

And, as they say, the rest is history. In fact, it was one of the pivotal moments in the history of Israel. However, it didn't look like significant history then.

A Mother's Sacrifice

What stood out most clearly was a mother's sacrifice. Hannah promised the Lord that, should she be granted a son, she would give the boy to the Lord "for his whole life" (1:28).

Many parents have stood at the altar of the church and given their child to the Lord. What's so special about what Hannah did? The parents of Samuel did far more than promise to raise a child in a religious atmosphere and try to keep him out of trouble. Samuel was given to the Lord to serve in the sanctuary soon after he was weaned from his mother's breast.

Hannah's sacrifice was greater than Elkanah's, and especially moving. In that day, parents depended on their children for security in old age. If Elkanah died, Hannah could not count on Peninnah nor her brood for help. She was on her own—unless she had a child, which she finally did. And then gave him away to God! But Hannah did not forget Samuel.

Samuel would have been at least three years of age when she gave him to serve in the sanctuary. Some scholars tell us he might have been five. Three or five years of love, prayer, and care prepared the lad for service before the Lord.

Nor did Hannah cut Samuel's limb off the family tree. "Each year [she] made him a little robe and took it to him when she went up with her husband to offer the annual sacrifice" (2:19).

Samuel's Call

"I never dreamed it would turn out like this." Those are not the words of Hannah, as far as we know. Still, they might have been had she lived long enough to see Samuel's impact on Israel. To a nation in despair, God sent a boy named Samuel, nurtured by a mother's love and taught by an aging priest.

Except possibly for Joshua, Samuel is the outstanding leader in Israel between Moses and David. He was Israel's last important judge and one of its earliest prophets. The Lord used him in the selection of Israel's first two kings. Through Samuel's influence, the faith and moral values that called Israel into being were built into the new governmental system when the people clamored for a king. Hannah and Elkanah could not have known, that fateful day at Shiloh, the eternal impact of their promise to give to God their yet-to-be-born son.

"And the boy Samuel continued to grow in stature and in favor with the LORD and with men" (2:26). Clearly the Lord knew Samuel had both the ability and the disposition to hear Him that early morning when He called.

The call of Samuel is a dramatic account in 3:1-10. He is called a boy, but that doesn't tell us how old he was. The Hebrew word used can mean an infant or 40-year-old adult. The term also is used to refer to a servant or personal attendant. We don't know how old the "boy" was, but that doesn't matter.

What does matter is that Samuel's home and temple life had prepared him for the call of God. There were some key people standing at this corner of Hebrew history nurturing Samuel. Hannah was there. And so was Elkanah. Eli was there as well, helping Samuel, even though he experienced heartache with his own sons.

A new day was dawning in Israel. Nevertheless, the sun would never rise without the sacrifice of some devoted parents and the vital contribution of a temple-based, nearly blind old man.

The Church as Family

In his story, we see how Samuel's "family" had prepared him to answer God's call and do God's work. His mother had prayed for him to come into existence. Then she gave Samuel back to God, allowing him to grow up and be taught in the temple. Eli, though a failure at raising his own sons, had the wisdom to recognize that it was God's voice calling Samuel, though such visitations were rare in those days (see 3:1). Eli also obviously taught Samuel to be a good priest. Samuel's association with Eli and the temple picked up the nurturing work of family where his mother and father left off.

There are four basic purposes or functions of family in today's society: having children; providing shelter, food, and clothing; caring for emotional needs (especially love); and educating children to live productively in society. The church functions like a family in similar ways. The church has children in the sense that it wins new converts through evangelism. Sometimes the church provides shelter, food, and clothing literally through charity work. At other times in a metaphorical sense of giving shelter from the storms of life and feeding on the Bread of Life (see John 6:35, 48). The church meets emotional needs through the loving fellowship of believers. And it provides education, often literally teaching persons to read or giving college scholarships, but also by making Christian disciples through the examples of faithful lives.

For families that are functioning well in basic purposes, the church is an extension of the family, providing love (in opportunities for divine worship and human fellowship) and education (growth in grace). All kinds of realities occur to families, such as death, divorce, remarriage that blends households, inability to have children, abuse, neglect, and so on. For persons touched by those circumstances, the church becomes a surrogate family, providing as much as possible a substitute for whatever is lacking in the biological family.

So, when we describe our congregation as a "family church," we are talking more about how it functions in people's lives than about the makeup of the families. The church, if it will, can act like a nurturing family to Christians, regardless of their particular life circumstances. The Anderson-like family (Mom, Dad, and two children) can find fulfilling fellowship and faith formation in the church family. So can the single-parent family and the single formerly married or never married person. All believers are thus a part of the family of God.

Families Have a Purpose

Samuel's story had wide implications for the nation of Israel. However, Samuel's life would not have been possible without the unique mixture of a devout mother and a teaching house of God.

Our families, in all the various forms we find them, have a

God-given purpose too. In a combined effort between biological parents and the church as a family, we are to create, nurture, love, and train a new generation of Christians. This happens best when we "family" each other as God through Christ "families" us.

Notes:

*Statistics for 2000 U.S. Census <www.factfinder.census.gov>. Statistics for 1950 U.S. Census <www.fisher.lib.virginia.edu>.

Scripture: 1 Samuel 1:1-2, 13-17, 28; 2:19, 26; 3:1-10; John 6:35, 48

A Glimpse of the Real World

Mary and Kevin were spending the afternoon at Grandma and Grandpa Christian's house. Kevin was intently coloring a picture in his favorite superhero coloring book. Suddenly, he was thirsty, so he left the room to get a glass of water.

Just then, his sister, Mary, walked into the room. She saw the open coloring book on the table and sat down to color a little of it.

Kevin came back into the room and saw Mary coloring. "Get away from my picture!" he yelled. When he saw how much Mary had done, with colors he didn't want to use, he started crying.

Grandma Christian came into the room to see what was the matter. Through his sobs, Kevin said, "She ruined my picture. She's always messing up my stuff. I hate her!"

"Now, now," Grandma soothed. "You shouldn't hate your sister over this." She turned to Mary. "Why did you do this?"

Mary looked at them sadly. "I . . . I just wanted to color a little. It used to make me feel good, when I was little, I guess. I'm really sorry, Kevin."

"See, Kevin. Mary didn't mean to destroy your picture. Couldn't you find it in your heart to forgive her?"

Kevin thought about it for a long minute. "I guess so."

"Good. Now you can start over with a brand-new picture, and color it just the way you like it."

As Mary left the room and Kevin set to work on a new picture, Grandma thought, *It is so easy to harbor grudges and to let hate grow in our hearts. Teaching children the way of forgiveness is one of the most important lessons we adults can offer. I hope God finds us all faithful in this responsibility.*

10

Starting Over

IS THERE ANYONE who has lived more than a few years who hasn't, at one time or another, felt like this poet?

> I wish there was some wonderful place
> Called the land of new beginning,
> Where all our mistakes and all our heartaches,
> All our poor, selfish griefs
> Might be dropped like a shabby old coat at the door
> And never put on again.
>
> —Louise Fletcher Tarkington

The Land of New Beginning is longed for most by those to whom it seems the farthest away. By all the people who cry out in the night, "If only I hadn't . . ." Like:

- The troubled teenager who can't go home.
- The divorced adult who has no one to go home to.
- The crushed victim of selfishness and sin.
- The casualty of destructive habits that seem unbreakable.

All these and more need a place to begin again.

Is the Land of Beginning Again mythical, just a fanciful wish without reality? Or does it exist in your congregation and in mine?

If such a place exists anywhere, it should be in the church. Our congregations should be about welcoming, forgiving, and restoring hurting persons. For if people don't find such acceptance in the church, they will look for it elsewhere. And many of the alternatives are bad places for them to be.

Sometimes it seems that the church has adopted a "one strike, you're out" policy. Violate a church rule once, and you get no second chance; you're marked for life. Often such an attitude is exhibited toward sinful behavior, but it can also be used against persons who even question their faith. It's like people may forgive the infraction, but they never quite forget. True restoration doesn't happen.

How can we expect to continue to pass on the Christian faith if we cannot create a welcoming place for those who wander or wonder? How should we treat those who leave the church and then want to return sometime later? What should be our approach to those who physically remain a part of the congregation but have serious questions about their faith?

In this chapter we want to examine these two areas that call for understanding—sin and doubt—to see how we can respond in ways that will restore persons to fellowship in the church. We want to answer the plaintive cry, "You're losing us," by creating a welcome place where no one needs to be lost.

Going Away and Coming Back

The Gospel of Luke records Jesus telling the parable of the lost son in 15:11-32. This is a story about a young man who left to do his own thing and later returned home. It is a study in how forgiveness works.

The young man in the parable made a decision to leave home, without knowing what lay ahead. No doubt he had dreams that things would be so much more exciting out in the free world than they were on his father's farm. There were places to see and people to meet. What an exciting prospect!

His father, though he surely knew that things would not be as his young son envisioned them, did not stop his departure. He gave his son what he asked, and watched him pack up and leave for parts unknown.

When the young man had spent all his money, had no so-called friends left, and was working at the most detestable job for a Jew—slopping hogs—he hit bottom. There, in his despair, he made a decision to return home. He expected to be rejected as a son. Nevertheless, he wanted to go home so badly he was willing to simply be a lowly servant on his father's land.

When the young man approached the homestead, he found his father waiting, watching for him, expecting him to come home. He not only was forgiven but also was restored to his place in the family as a son.

Why was home such a welcoming place? Because of his father's attitude. When the young man left, his father never gave up the expectation that one day he would return. He did not write him off or disown him. He waited patiently, hopefully, fully prepared to forgive when he returned.

However, note the older brother's attitude. He was not forgiving. He resented the restoration of his brother because he had been the steady one who stayed home while his brother wasted his life and resources. The whole situation made the older brother angry.

The difference in the father's and the older son's attitudes in this parable raises two questions pertinent to our inquiry today. First, what creates a welcoming atmosphere in church? Second, what hinders forgiveness and restoration?

The lost son's father created a forgiving atmosphere by his attitude. He *expected* the son to return. He *expected* to forgive him. His only difficulty was waiting (patiently?) for the reunion day to come, for his son to start on his way back home.

The lessons of this parable are consistent with Jesus' more explicit teaching about forgiveness. In a portion of the Sermon on the Mount, Jesus set up a tit-for-tat condition. However, His focus was on forgiveness, not revenge. "If you forgive men when they sin against you, your heavenly Father will also forgive you. But if you do not forgive men their sins, your Father will not forgive your sins" (Matthew 6:14-15). Jesus made it clear that our own forgiveness will be no more or no less than the forgiveness we show others.

Later Peter, like many of us, wanted Jesus to establish some guideline so he could be certain that he had done enough on this matter. So Peter, thinking he was being more than generous, asked, "Lord, how many times shall I forgive my brother when he sins against me? Up to seven times?" (18:21).

However, Jesus opened the concept up beyond what Peter could imagine. "Jesus answered, 'I tell you, not seven times, but seventy-seven times'" (v. 22). "Seventy-seven times" could also be translated "seventy times seven" or 490 times. Regardless, 77 times is more than enough, more times than one person will ask to be forgiven. We need to maintain an open-ended account for each person when it comes to forgiveness.

The apostle Paul also practiced what Jesus preached. He gave this advice to the Christians at Corinth regarding any among their number who had sinned. "You ought to forgive and comfort him, so that he will not be overwhelmed by excessive sorrow. I urge you . . . to reaffirm your love for him" (2 Corinthians 2:7-8). Paul was concerned with the effect nonforgiveness would have on the person—too much grief to handle and that awful feeling of not being loved.

In his letter to the Colossians, Paul echoed Jesus' explicit teaching as the way to keep peace within the congregation. "Bear with each other and forgive whatever grievances you may have against one another. Forgive as the Lord forgave you" (3:13). Those who have experienced forgiveness from the Lord should be most open to extending forgiveness to others. They know how good it feels.

What hinders a church from being a welcoming place of restoration? At least two factors negatively affect a congregation: being only self-interested and being judgmental.

Paul wrote to Timothy and predicted how self-absorption among the culture could affect Christian congregations in the future. "There will be terrible times in the last days. People will be lovers of themselves, lovers of money, boastful, proud, abusive, . . . *without love, unforgiving,* . . . conceited, lovers of pleasure rather than lovers of God—having a form of godliness but denying its power. Have nothing to do with them" (2 Timothy 3:1-5, emphasis added). Has this happened in any churches already? God forbid!

Jesus addressed the issue of being judgmental, again in a "what you give is what you get" formulation. "Do not judge, and you will not be judged. Do not condemn, and you will not be condemned. Forgive, and you will be forgiven" (Luke 6:37).

Jesus did not mean by this that we are not to be discerning, that we are to accept anything and everything that comes along. He does not want us to be judges, but He does expect us to be fruit inspectors. "A good tree cannot bear bad fruit, and a bad tree cannot bear good fruit. . . . Thus, by their fruit you will recognize them" (Matthew 7:18, 20). Jesus knew how the world is. That is why He said, "I am sending you out like sheep among wolves. Therefore be as shrewd as snakes and as innocent as doves" (10:16).

We are not to judge or condemn anyone, for those decisions belong to God alone. "[God] commands all people everywhere to repent. For he has set a day when he will judge the world with justice by the man he has appointed" (Acts 17:30-31). God is the only one who can do this fairly, for only He knows all the facts and circumstances.

From a human illustration, there is a difference in a courtroom between a judge's perspective and a mother's view of the accused. The judge will review the case, make a ruling of guilt, and sentence the person to punishment. Then the judge is finished. He or she is probably not interested in the accused any longer.

The accused person's mother, on the other hand, also believes that if her son or daughter is guilty, he or she should suffer punishment. However, the mother still loves the accused.

The judge is interested solely in justice, the punishment fitting the crime. No matter how contrite the accused may be, the judge is only interested in him or her suffering a punishment befitting the crime. The mother is interested in the continued welfare of the person she loves. She wants to restore that son or daughter to his or her former place. Her attitude will create more of a welcoming space for rehabilitation than the judge's attitude of punishment and indifference to the person.

Jesus wants us to act like mothers of accused persons and fathers of lost sons rather than judges who condemn and only mete out punishment. God is always looking for any indication that a person is turning toward Him. It is up to us to create an atmosphere in every congregation that encourages such steps toward God.

Doubting and Believing

Sometimes people do not leave a congregation physically and go out into sin. Rather, their struggle is with doubts about the faith. How does or should the church treat such persons? Do their honest questions undermine the faith, or are they signs of genuine interest in Christianity?

I must confess, I feel sorry for Thomas. He was one of the elite 12, the disciples handpicked by Jesus. Yet, I think he has had a bad rap all these years. We know him as "doubting" Thomas.

Peter and John didn't believe the Resurrection had occurred until they saw the empty tomb and graveclothes. Yet, we don't call them doubters for that time between Mary's announcement to them and their seeing the evidence in the tomb.

Jesus himself showed the other disciples "his hands and side" (John 20:20). That was the same evidence Thomas, who for some reason had missed that Sunday evening service, asked for in order to be convinced Jesus was alive.

When Jesus appeared again a week later, Thomas was at the meeting. However, Jesus did not chide Thomas. He simply offered Thomas what he needed for faith.

Lots of people are like Thomas. They have questions about Christianity, but those uncertainties are part of their desire to be certain of the truth. They do not need our chiding them to "just believe." They need understanding—and answers.

Of course, as soon as we pull out our Bibles to explore what attitude we should have toward doubts, we run smack into tension. When we turn to Jude, we read, "Be merciful to those who doubt" (v. 22). When we turn to what James had to say, we see that he recognized who has the answers to our doubts. "If any of you lacks wisdom, he should ask God, who gives generously to all without finding fault" (1:5). And he revealed God's attitude toward those who doubt—generosity and not finding fault.

However, in the verses immediately following that comforting advice, James took a dim view of doubting. "But when he asks, he must believe and not doubt, because he who doubts is like a wave of the sea, blown and tossed by the wind. That man should not think he will receive anything from the Lord; he is a double-minded man, unstable in all he does" (vv. 6-8).

Do we have conflicting views about doubt here? Does Jude's telling us to be merciful contradict James's warning about doubt making for instability? Are Jude and James talking about the same doubt Jesus meant when He told Thomas, "Stop doubting and believe" (John 20:27)?

It becomes clear when we look at the Greek words, all of which are translated "doubt" in the NIV. Both Jude and James used a word that implies wavering. Jesus used a different word that means unbelief. James is correct that the person who wavers in his or her faith tends to be unstable. It is better to ask God for the wisdom to more firmly believe. Such persons do not struggle with not believing in God so much as wavering in their faith as they hear various opinions put forward. Some people are just confused by what they hear.

Jude appeals to us to be gentle with such people. His sentiments echo Paul's, who believed that Christians should exhibit such characteristics all the time. "Be completely humble and gentle; be patient, bearing with one another in love" (Ephesians 4:2). Paul also advised, "Accept him whose faith is weak, without passing judgment on disputable matters" (Romans 14:1).

Thomas's doubt was not a wavering between two opinions. Thomas was without faith in the Resurrection; he did not believe Jesus had risen. Jesus urged him to move from not believing to believing. However, He did it in a gentle way. Jesus did not use scolding language with Thomas as He had done with the Pharisees who tried to trap Him with their unbelieving questions. He was willing to give Thomas whatever proof he needed. "Put your finger here; see my hands. Reach out your hand and put it into my side" (John 20:27).

Thomas did not need to touch Jesus to make the move from unbelief in the Resurrection to believing this was the risen Lord standing in front of him. If we are gentle with those who question their faith and patiently try to provide them whatever proof they need, we will create an accepting atmosphere in which they will find it easier to believe and not waver. And the entire Body of Believers will grow.

Conclusion

Remember the Land of New Beginning we mentioned at the start of this chapter? Can we agree now that the church is and should be that place?

When we have a patient and expectant attitude toward those who sin and leave the church, we create a safe haven to which they can come back to experience God's love. When we are willing to forgive 77 times or 490 times, people will not hesitate to seek God's forgiveness in our congregation.

When we can gently bear with those among us whose faith is weak or wavering, we keep strife to a minimum and spiritual growth to a maximum.

Those may be just the Christian attitudes the next generation needs to be convinced not to leave to look for greener pastures outside the church. That would be worth far more than we could ever imagine.

Scripture: Matthew 6:14-15; 7:18, 20; 10:16; 18:21-22; Luke 6:37; 15:11-32; John 20:20, 27; Acts 17:30-31; Romans 14:1; 2 Corinthians 2:7-8; Ephesians 4:2; Colossians 3:13; 2 Timothy 3:1-5; James 1:5-8; Jude 22

A Glimpse of the Real World

The doorbell rang at the Christians' home. Bob answered it and found a well-dressed couple standing on the porch.

"Hello," the man said kindly. "We're out visiting some of our neighbors today to tell them about Jesus. May I ask what church your family attends?"

"We go to Pleasant Street Church," Bob replied.

"Do you know Jesus as your Savior?"

"Yes, I'm glad to say we do."

"Praise the Lord," the man said. "Then we won't take up any more of your time. Have a good day." The couple walked down the sidewalk and headed for the neighbor's house.

As he closed the door, Bob turned to find his entire family standing behind him.

"What did they want?" his wife, Betty, asked.

"They are just going door-to-door, telling people about Jesus."

Kevin piped up, "Cool! That'd be fun. I'd like to tell everyone about Jesus like that."

His sister, Mary, wasn't as enthusiastic. "I think it'd be way cooler to become a soccer star and then give my testimony on TV. A whole lot more people would hear about Jesus that way."

Their older brother, Bobby, made a sniffing sound. "No way! People are always watching everything we do anyway. They can just watch me and tell if I'm a Christian. I don't want to talk to any of my friends about Jesus. I don't want to be some kind of Jesus nerd."

Bob caught Betty's eyes as their children spouted their opinions. "Someone needs to tell the gospel story," Bob said. Yet the incident left a question in his mind: *What is the best way for my children to understand what it means to witness?*

11

Telling the Story

D ADDY, TELL ME a story."
    That is not an intimidating request. In fact, telling a child a bedtime story is really a pleasurable event.

When my daughter was small, those were her words most nights. We would sit on her four-poster, canopied bed and read from one of two books: *Little Visits with God* or *More Little Visits with God*. They told the Bible stories in language a five-year-old could understand.

"Christian, witness for Me."

Now that *is* an intimidating request. Yet it need not be. Witnessing isn't really any more difficult than reading Bible stories to a child if we understand what witnessing really is. Witnessing is simply sharing what we believe in ways that others understand.

In this chapter, we will examine the importance of witnessing to our faith and its impact on the next generation. Then we will look at how we share the gospel both outside and inside the community of faith.

The Importance of Sharing

We would be hard-pressed to find a Christian who does not think that witnessing to the faith is important. Nevertheless, we would be just as hard-pressed to find many Christians who actually witness. We are intimidated by the very word. No one looks forward to being a witness in a court case; lawyers can be awfully tough with their questions. When it comes to witnessing for Christ, most of us are afraid that the person to whom we are talking might be as tough as a cross-examining lawyer.

Despite our negative associations with the word "witness," sharing the Good News is an important responsibility (and privilege) for Christians. There are several reasons for this mandate.

Jesus modeled how to witness. When John the Baptist sent two of his disciples to Jesus to ask if He was the Messiah, Jesus pointed to His ministry as a witness: "Go back and report to John what you have seen and heard: The blind receive sight, the lame walk, those who have leprosy are cured, the deaf hear, the dead are raised, and the good news is preached to the poor" (Luke 7:22). These were all things that only the Anointed One of God could do, so they were striking evidences that Jesus was indeed the Messiah.

However, the principle laid down by Jesus is found in the words, "report . . . what you have seen and heard." Honest witnesses do not make up the stories they tell. Rather, they recount actual experiences they have had. Here, Jesus was telling John's two disciples to tell him what they themselves had seen and heard as they followed Him around Judea.

Witnessing is important because *Jesus commanded it*. When Jesus appeared to the 11 remaining disciples on the evening of the day He was resurrected, He explained the Scriptures to them. He indicated that this was the gospel that would be the basis for the disciples' preaching. "This is what is written: The Christ will suffer and rise from the dead on the third day, and repentance and forgiveness of sins will be preached in his name to all nations, beginning at Jerusalem. You are witnesses of these things" (Luke 24:46-48).

The risen Lord's interaction with the disciples continued. "He appeared to them over a period of forty days" (Acts 1:3). Then He specifically laid out His plans for them and for all disciples. "You will be my witnesses in Jerusalem, and in all Judea and Samaria, and to the ends of the earth" (v. 8).

Picking up the command of Jesus after the Day of Pentecost, *the disciples taught witnessing.* In several sermons throughout the Book of Acts, Peter affirmed that the disciples were indeed witnesses for Christ. On one occasion at Cornelius's house, Peter said, "We are witnesses of everything [Jesus] did in the country of the Jews and in Jerusalem. They killed him by hanging him on a tree, but God raised him from the dead on the third day and caused him to be seen" (10:39-40).

Much later when writing a letter, John gave a wonderful reason to the Christian community for sharing the Good News. "We proclaim to you what we have seen and heard, so that you also may have fellowship with us. And our fellowship is with the Father and with his Son, Jesus Christ" (1 John 1:3). Witnessing draws persons into blessed communion with the Church and with the Triune God.

Witnesses simply share their actual experiences. It is a natural result of sharing our lives with each other. As Peter and John told the Sanhedrin, "We cannot help speaking about what we have seen and heard" (Acts 4:20). That should be every Christian's feeling as we share the story of Jesus everywhere, in ever-widening circles from Jerusalem to the ends of the earth.

Sharing the Story

The Church has an evangelistic responsibility to the world at large, namely, to tell the good news of salvation that Jesus Christ has brought to all of humanity. The Church fulfills that obligation as it witnesses to its experience of the risen Lord. However, the job of witnessing to the world is not necessarily an easy one. The world, absorbed in its own ideas and pursuit of pleasure, often does not want to hear what Christians have to say.

This is nothing new, not a modern problem only. It has been the case from the first days of the Early Church. Peter addressed the issue with words of encouragement in his first letter. He knew from firsthand experience what it was like to be persecuted for relating "what we have seen and heard" (Acts 4:20). Therefore, he wrote, "'Do not fear what they fear; do not be frightened.' But in your hearts set apart Christ as Lord. Always be prepared to give an answer to everyone who asks you to give the reason for the hope that you have. But do this with gentleness and respect, keeping a clear conscience, so that those who speak maliciously against your good behavior in Christ may be ashamed of their slander" (1 Peter 3:14-16).

Fear is probably the main thing that keeps most Christians from actively witnessing to their faith. In fact, many who are reading these words right now can feel the tension rising in them as they think about the subject of evangelism. However, they can relax if they simply remember that the Holy Spirit's strength overcomes human weakness.

In reality, we do not need to be fearful. We already know the story from personal experience. We have individually and personally become Christians and walked with Christ. Prepared by that wealth of knowledge, we can simply share our own story, the story of how the gospel of Jesus Christ changed our lives. How hard can it be to explain to someone what you have personally experienced? That takes a little of the fear out, doesn't it?

Also, we need not be fearful because we do not witness merely from our own strength. The Holy Spirit is within us, to lead us to people to whom to witness and to guide us in the process of sharing the gospel. The Holy Spirit's power overcomes our human weaknesses and shortcomings. The Holy Spirit can take our fumbling words and clearly impress the message of the gospel upon the hungry hearer's heart.

There are two important characteristics the Holy Spirit will help us maintain as we share the gospel. "Gentleness and respect" (v. 15) go better with the message of the gospel than other methods. We have all seen instances where a witness for Christ was not gentle or respectful, so we were not surprised when the message was not received or the one witnessing was counterattacked.

Witnessing not only is telling strangers about Christ but also has an internal component in the Church—reminding ourselves of the gospel message and telling our faith stories to each other. Even the Early Church began their witnessing at home in

Jerusalem before they scattered throughout the known world (see Acts 8:1).

Telling the gospel story within the church reinforces our hope in Christ. No matter how many times we repeat this, it is encouraging to hear a congregation affirming, "Christ has died. Christ is risen. Christ will come again." In a myriad of ways—Sunday School classes, Bible studies, Vacation Bible Schools, and even potluck dinners—we repeat and live out the gospel message. And our children surely take notice of what we say and do.

Others in the group, especially the children, won't know our personal faith stories unless we tell them. We need to find creative ways to share our stories of conversion, because not many churches have "testimony time" anymore. Some people may not have told their own conversion story for years. Simply sharing how we came to faith and where we are in our present walk with the Lord is important and meaningful.

In finding creative ways to share the gospel story with each other and telling our personal conversion stories, we practice for witnessing to those outside the church. As the saying goes, "Practice makes perfect." We may not become perfect witnesses, but we will certainly hone our skills with intentional repetition.

Ways of Sharing

If we follow Peter's advice by not being fearful, always being prepared to share, and remaining gentle and respectful in our approach, we will be effective witnesses. However, there is more than one way to go about the task. Let's briefly review five such methods.

Confrontation-persuasion. Many consider this the *only* method of evangelism. People think of this as the famous "buttonhole" tactic—pin someone down and make him or her listen to your presentation of the gospel. And this is the most fear-inducing because such tactics would (and probably should) create great resistance. No one likes to be bullied, and especially not bullied into becoming a Christian.

However, persuasion evangelism need not be so confrontational. There are times when we need to be intentional about helping someone make a decision for Christ, but there is no reason to forget to be gentle and respectful in the process. Intentionality and direction do not require heavy-handed tactics. Kind and gentle leading is more Christlike.

Intellectual-apologetic. This kind of witness usually takes the form of writing books, magazine articles, or gospel tracts. College professors, Christian publishers, many preachers, and the New Testament writers are some of the people God calls to this kind of evangelism. Though the number of persons involved may not be large, still this is an important ministry with eternal purposes. As Luke stated in his Gospel, "Since I myself have carefully investigated everything from the beginning, it seemed good . . . to write an orderly account . . . *so that you may know the certainty of the things you have been taught*" (1:3-4, emphasis added). John, in reporting the numerous miracles Jesus did, said, "These are written that you may believe that Jesus is the Christ, the Son of God, and that by believing you may have life in his name" (John 20:31).

Bible study. Another effective means of witnessing that some Christians use is inviting persons into their homes for Bible studies. One thing that makes this method more attractive to nonchurched persons is that someone's home seems like a more neutral setting than the church building. Therefore, they feel freer to participate, and in doing so hear the gospel.

Compassion. Many Christians find ways to do good deeds for others, and then point to Christ as the motivation behind their actions. This often takes the form of helping those in need, and fulfills Jesus' teaching about caring for others. In the middle of a discussion about feeding the hungry, giving a drink to the thirsty, inviting the stranger to come inside, clothing the naked, and visiting the sick and imprisoned, Jesus made our motive clear. "Whatever you did for one of the least of these brothers of mine, you did for me" (Matthew 25:40).

Inviting people to attend church with us. Many folks might not consider this witnessing, but it is. It is not as explicit as sharing your testimony or writing a faith statement or even doing good deeds for others. Nevertheless, it reflects your vision of the church as a place where people can find forgiveness and restoration, and that is a witness for Christ in itself.

The above five methods are only a few of the many ways Christians can share their faith with others. There is no stereotype for effective witnessing. One evangelism expert has estimated that anywhere from 1 to 10 persons show love in various ways before an individual reaches the point of converting to Christianity. So, there are 1 to 10 or even more ways to witness to that person—creative, Spirit-led practices that will "warm the person up for the gospel."[1] We simply need to actively seek to discover which way is best for us to share our faith with the rest of the world.

Simply Sharing

Sometimes the way we share will not even seem like witnessing. That is the lesson one author learned. She wrote:

When I became a Christian, I determined to share my faith, never missing opportunities to witness to people I'd meet in supermarkets, on the job, my family, and friends. I thought the only way for me to be effective would be to *tell* another person of the plan of salvation through Jesus. Imagine my surprise when I learned there is yet another way to witness.

My husband and I were admiring our new son when a patient was wheeled into my hospital room and placed in the bed by the window. "Vi had a baby girl," the nurse said as she introduced us.

This was Vi's first child, while we were welcoming our fifth. *We have little in common,* I thought. *What will we talk about in the next days?* Yet, I turned my face toward the pillow and whispered, "Help me, God, to be a bold witness to Vi."

An inner voice seemed to say, "I don't want you to witness to her."

That was all. I wondered what the words meant.

That evening, Vi and I fed our babies and settled in for the night. Except for an occasional cry from the nursery, all was quiet. After the lights were dimmed, we began to talk, and our conversation quickly turned to Vi's family and friends.

"My mom and dad love me. I know they do," she said. "It's just that they're . . . they're so *busy*."

She went on to tell how her teen years had been a struggle for acceptance. Her parents, giving attention to her more talented siblings, seemed unaware of their quieter daughter's needs. Desperate, Vi turned to an older man for attention, and now she had borne his child.

"Phil is so nice to me," she said. "I don't know why he didn't come . . ." Her voice trailed off. "But now I have the baby. It's going to be so much fun to take care of her."

The next two days were filled with visitors "oohing" over our babies, but when evenings came, Vi talked and I listened.

I learned a lot about witnessing those evenings. I discovered that witnessing may be talking to people about Christ. That's important, but equally important are the times when I listen to the deepest heart-cry of another person. In those times, I am one link in the chain that will eventually help the person connect to God. That, too, is witnessing.

After three days, Vi and I said good-bye, each reluctant to break off our friendship. As the nurse wheeled me down the hall, I buried my face in the soft bundle in my arms.

"Lord, I didn't outline the plan of salvation for Vi," I murmured. "I didn't pray with her. I didn't share a scripture verse."

"But you did listen to her," He reminded me. "You did show love. And that's the greatest witness of all."[2]

Many Ways, One Goal

In this discussion, we have seen that witnessing to our Christian faith is not limited to one method. If we are listening and willing, the Spirit will show us how to witness appropriately in each situation.

Our children learn easily and can readily create new ways to tackle important tasks. As they watch us witness to our faith in a variety of settings, they will learn that sharing the gospel story with others is an integral part of who we are as Christians. And they will be free to find methods to spread the message in ways that their peers can understand and accept.

The next generation will be won to the Lord as our children continue telling the story of the transforming gospel of Jesus Christ.

Notes:

1. Lyle Pointer, "Starting Spiritual Conversations," *Skill Builder Video Series* (Kansas City: WordAction, 2001).

2. Jewell Johnson, "The Greatest Witness," *Standard*, May 4, 2003. Used by permission. All rights reserved.

Scripture: Matthew 25:40; Luke 1:3-4; 7:22; 24:46-48; John 20:31; Acts 1:3, 8; 4:20; 8:1; 10:39-40; 1 Peter 3:14-16; 1 John 1:3

A Glimpse of the Real World

As he listened to his children talk about their day at school, Bob Christian realized something. He said to his wife, Betty, "Things sure have changed since we were in school."

"They sure have," she agreed.

"Like how?" asked Bobby.

"Well," Bob began. "Mary said she wished she knew Spanish because all the new kids are from Mexico. When I was in school, the only Spanish we ever heard was what the Spanish teacher said. And we didn't have to understand her to pass the class."

"And Kevin talked about a kid named Rasheed or Rashim," interjected Betty. "His family is Hindu or Muslim or something. I had never heard of those religions when I was in school. Everybody in my class was just like me."

"Not anymore!" exclaimed Bobby. "The kids in my class are all kinds of religions besides Christian—Muslims, Hindus, Jews, and even a few who say they don't believe in God."

Things sure are different, Bob thought. *The world my kids are in has spiritual challenges my generation never even thought about.*

12

The Faces Around Us

THE MISSIONARY'S plea for finances to educate children in Africa stirred Ed to the depths. He took a $20 bill from his wallet, the first of many contributions he made to support the mission school.

Two months later when a Christian ex-gang leader challenged Ed to support a community ministry aimed at educating and evangelizing inner-city children, Ed expressed indignation. "Those good-for-nothing kids are ruining our community. They'll never get one dime of my money!"

How could Ed feel this way? The children in Africa pose no personal threat to Ed or his way of life. The children in his town have the potential to change things for the worse, so Ed feels.

How do we respond to the fact that the world has come to us? That they live in our neighborhood, on our street? How will our reaction affect the future of our church and our ability to influence the next generation?

In order to answer those questions, we can first see how the Jerusalem church handled new circumstances. Then we can take a look at some of the new faces around us.

The First Church Discussion

Paul and Barnabas were traveling around the area we know

today as Turkey and Syria, preaching the gospel of Jesus Christ, and performing "miraculous signs and wonders" (Acts 14:3). Everywhere they went, they made some new converts to Christianity and found resistance from other persons. In Iconium, the disgruntled Gentiles and Jews formed a plot to stone them. Paul and Barnabas found out about it and fled to Lystra. In that city the miracles caused the crowds to think they were Greek gods come to life. It was all Paul could do to keep them from offering sacrifices to them as gods. Nevertheless, Paul could not keep them from stoning him and leaving him for dead.

Paul revived. He and Barnabas traveled to Derbe and "preached the good news in that city and won a large number of disciples" (v. 21). Then they made another round of the cities of that region, "strengthening the disciples and encouraging them to remain true to the faith" (v. 22), and then sailed to Attalia. From Attalia they went back to Antioch in Syria and "stayed there a long time with the disciples" (v. 28).

The Church was spreading far beyond the confines of Jerusalem. With all the Gentile converts, the membership was changing. No longer were there only Christian Jews; now the Church had converts with all kinds of backgrounds. Some of the Jerusalem Christians came down to Antioch and taught that a person had to become a Jew (that is, "circumcised, according to the custom taught by Moses" [15:1]) in order to be saved. Jesus was a Jew. The first converts were Jews. It seemed only natural to them that all future Christians should also be Jews.

To say this caused a difference of opinion would be putting it mildly. The Bible describes it this way: "This brought Paul and Barnabas into sharp dispute and debate with [those teachers]" (v. 2a). This was a serious matter, one that had great impact on the future course of the Church.

"So Paul and Barnabas were appointed, along with some other believers, to go up to Jerusalem to see the apostles and elders about this question" (v. 2b). Thus, the first discussion of an important matter of potential change happened.

The Scriptures don't give us many details about what went

on at the meeting, but we do know a few things, including the conclusion they reached.

We know that the Christians who belonged to the Pharisee party supported the teaching that "the Gentiles must be circumcised and required to obey the law of Moses" (v. 5). They might even have felt they had Jesus on their side. They could have quoted Him saying, "Salvation is from the Jews" (John 4:22).

The "apostles and elders" (Acts 15:6) then had a discussion meeting. We don't know what went on there—no minutes were recorded in the Bible—but we do have Peter's concluding remarks. Peter said, in effect, why make the new people do what we can't do ourselves (see vv. 10, also 19)? Though they had all been good Jews like their fathers before them, following the letter of Moses' law did not bring them salvation. Rather, Peter pointed out, "We believe it is through the grace of our Lord Jesus that we are saved, just as [the Gentiles] are" (v. 11).

The question they were trying to answer in this debate was an important one. Is Christianity for all people everywhere? If it is not, why evangelize outside Jerusalem? Yet there seemed to be definite clues that Christianity was meant for everyone. In John 3:16 Jesus used an unqualified "whoever" to say that believers in Him would have eternal life. In John 10:16 He enigmatically referred to "other sheep" about whom He was concerned: "I must bring them also. They too will listen to my voice, and there shall be one flock." As He was ascending into heaven, Jesus charged His disciples with a mission that would take them "to the ends of the earth" (Acts 1:8). When John was being shown heaven, he heard a song that worshiped Jesus, the Lamb of God: "With your blood you purchased men for God from every tribe and language and people and nation" (Revelation 5:9).

After Peter's speech, Paul and Barnabas affirmed what God was doing among the Gentiles. Then James spoke up and named four things to retain out of the law, and not to saddle the new people with the rest of the Jewish regulations. James said, "We should write to them, telling them to abstain from food polluted by idols, from sexual immorality, from the meat of strangled ani-

mals and from blood" (Acts 15:20). In other words, as long as
they stay away from impurity, they should be welcome among us.
The new people need not become practicing Jews to be Christians, but they should be pure in their relationship to God. Idols,
sexual immorality, and impurity in food were blocks to holiness;
nothing else about the new people would get in the way.

This settlement allowed everyone to win. The Jewish
Christians were not threatened with impurity by accepting the
Gentiles. The new people were not burdened with an impossible
task of trying to keep 613 Jewish regulations. And the work of
the Church, the spread of the good news about Jesus, could continue.

New Faces Around Us

A congregation builds a beautiful church building in a nice
section of town. As the years go by, the neighborhood changes.
Old people move out; new people move in. The ones the church
was built to serve are no longer in the area. Then the congregation has three choices: move to a new neighborhood, adapt to
the changes, or close the church.

I would suspect that most congregations would choose to
adapt to the changes. Their compassionate hearts would cause
them to try to reach out in love to whoever lives in the neighborhood. Yet it doesn't take long under changed conditions to
hear someone say something like this:

- "Nothing's the same anymore. We didn't use to have
  these problems."
- "Too many new groups are using our building; we can't
  keep it clean."
- "I can't understand a thing they say. They need to go
  where someone speaks their language."
- "There's just no helping some people."
- "Their bad habits will rub off on our children. We have
  to maintain some standards."

These are complaints, aimed at trying to keep the new people out because "they're not like us." It would be only one more

short step to insist, like the Pharisees in the Jerusalem church, that the new people become "just like us" or leave.

Embracing Change

Change happens, and we need to embrace it.

What are some of the barriers to reaching across cultures? Basically, the same ones as reaching across generations.

Language differences. There are now more than 250 languages spoken in the United States.[1] According to a recent census, approximately 32 million (14 percent of the population) do not speak English. More than half of them (17 million) speak Spanish. Another 6 million speak four major languages (in descending order): French, German, Italian, and Chinese.[2] The rest speak the other languages and dialects.

How many of those top five foreign languages has your congregation tried to learn recently?

The next generation's slang can seem just as foreign as any other language. It may not be necessary for the older generation to learn to talk like the kids, but it is important that we learn to communicate with them in ways they understand.

Cultural practices. When immigrants come here from their homelands, they bring their customs with them. Often those practices will seem strange to us. However, applying James's rule, if the custom does not defile holiness, we can often accommodate it.

Certain behavior is considered normal within a culture, even within the subculture of a younger generation. Some of those practices may get in the way of being Christian; others may not. It is our job to sort out the difference. That is no small task.

Looks and clothes. Native costumes are often exotic and colorful. Skin colors and eye shapes are as varied as anything else in nature. We must learn to live with what we call "unusual" clothes and different pigments if we are to welcome the new people into the fold of Christianity.

By the same token, we must learn to accept that the young people do not dress as we do.

One author made this point in a story about a young man

named Trent. "He looked like a cartoon character. His Mohawk haircut was bad enough—it was dyed fuchsia—but a large, green fish dangled from the lobe of one ear."

It took her aging father to help her understand the strange boy. "Trent is reaching young people who may not step foot inside a church and probably would not go to his band concerts if he played old-style hymns. . . . He is luring them to God's love, using his own music style and looks."[3]

Our evangelization to the next generation may not require accepting such drastic looks, but it might. Are we prepared to see what is important in packages that might look strange?

Our level of desire to reach out. This may be the most important key. We can overcome the other barriers more easily if our desire to share the Christian faith across cultures and generations is strong. The more we want to see others come to Christ, the more we can tolerate the nonessential differences between them and us.

What Can We Do?

That's a good question to ask. We can get involved in the lives of people from other cultures (who may be living right in our neighborhoods) and in the next generation of Christians (who are living with us right now). What are some of the ways we can overcome the differences between others and ourselves so that they can see Christ working in us?

Here is a partial list of suggested involvement:

- Become knowledgeable and work on migrant worker and immigration issues.
- Become aware of employment-related issues of both neighborhood persons and teenagers of the church.
- Look for opportunities to help with voter registration and education about political issues.
- Become involved in social issues of the community.
- Provide classes for health education.
- Teach children and/or adults to read.
- Tutor children with their school lessons.

- Provide space and support for a substance-abuse recovery program.
- Start an adult daycare center and preschool or after-school care.
- Begin a prison ministry.
- Build housing for the elderly.
- Become aware of senior citizen issues.
- Start a Christian counseling center or crisis hotline.
- Build a hospital or nursing home facilities.
- Operate a thrift store.
- Stock a pantry for emergency food assistance.
- Provide cash assistance for specific needs.

If we get involved in any of the above, we will meet a wide diversity of people. And we will often have opportunities to share Christ with them. As the old saying goes, "They don't care how much you know until they know how much you care." The above examples are only some of the ways we can show people we care.

And as our children watch us being involved with other people in these ways, or even join us in these efforts, they will catch the vision Jesus cast when He told the parable about separating the sheep and the goats:

> "The righteous will answer him, 'Lord, when did we see you hungry and feed you, or thirsty and give you something to drink? When did we see you a stranger and invite you in, or needing clothes and clothe you? When did we see you sick or in prison and go to visit you?'

> "The King will reply, 'I tell you the truth, whatever you did for one of the least of these brothers of mine, you did for me'" (Matthew 25:37-40).

Compassionate acts allow us to put our belief into action. As James wrote, "As the body without the spirit is dead, so faith without deeds is dead" (2:26). In the midst of doing those things Jesus commanded us to do for others, we will learn that the strange faces around us belong to real people for whom Christ also died.

Into the Future

It is easier to send money to faraway missionaries than to invest our lives in the people in our neighborhoods. It is hard to deal with differences in cultures and generations right under our noses. We wonder if assimilating different cultural and age-groups will destroy our faith or the church. Or must we insist that the new people become exactly like us in order to be part of the church?

Did accepting new people destroy the Early Church? No. Here's what they did:

- They kept salvation by grace through faith in Christ central in their message.
- They respected each other's differences and faced them in a spirit of prayer guided by the Holy Spirit.
- They were willing to make adjustments to their religious practices as the gospel reached new racial and cultural groups.
- They accepted some limitations in the way they lived in order to help those who had strong feelings on certain issues.
- Everyone, even the Jewish conservatives, supported the final decision. There was a beautiful spirit of unity in diversity.

We can see that our neighborhoods are changing. The world that was once foreign to us has moved to where we live. As this trend continues, our children will grow up in a diverse culture we never imagined. Whether the different cultures will dilute Christianity, or even replace it, depends on what we do now.

What lesson can we learn from the way the Early Church wrestled with these issues? Each congregation must assess who its new neighbors are and how it needs to reach them. Then find ways—even adapting to new ways—to bring them to Christ.

Christ is still the Savior of the world—whether the people of the world are in faraway countries or right at our doorstep. The good news of the Christian message is that Christ can bring salvation to every person who will accept Him. For our children's sake and the sake of the gospel, let us find ways to bring God's transforming love to the changing world in which we live.

Notes:

1. Sondra Thiederman, "Overcome Language Barriers: Get Your Message Across to Non-English Speakers,"
<www.equalopportunity.monster,com/articles>.

2. <www.census.gov/population/socdemo/language/table5>.

3. Mary Groves, "Fish Bait," *Standard*, November 17, 2002. Used by permission. All rights reserved.

Scripture: Matthew 25:37-40; John 3:16; 4:22; 10:16; Acts 1:8; 14:3, 21-22, 28; 15:1-22; James 2:26; Revelation 5:9

A Glimpse of the Real World

The hour was late. All three of the children had gone to bed. Bob pushed the off button on the TV remote, and the house was finally quiet. He and Betty sat together on the couch, enjoying the stillness.

"You know, Betty," Bob began. "I really don't know what to do."

"About what?" Betty asked, without raising her head from its comfortable place on Bob's shoulder.

"About teaching the kids. I want them to grow up in the church."

"We go to church every Sunday. They *are* growing up in the church," Betty interjected.

"I know. I mean I want them to grow up in the church and have a vital faith in Christ. I don't want them to fail to see the importance of our faith and drift away from the church and the Lord."

"Do you mean, as Bobby seems to be doing?"

"Right. He's at that critical age when he's questioning everything. I don't want him to turn his back on Christianity and go after all the empty, destructive things the world offers."

Betty agreed. "And we don't want Mary and Kevin doing that when they hit their teenage years either. You're right. We need to do something, and we need to do it now. In just a few years, it will be too late."

"I know. But what can we do?"

They both drifted back into the silence, prayerfully thinking about how to keep from losing their kids.

Let's Do Something!

TEN YEARS may seem like a long time, a long way into the future. Yet, in 10 years many of the things we enjoy or the opportunities we have now will be gone.

See that 7-year-old throwing a baseball with you in the backyard? In 10 years he'll be 17 and packing to go away to college.

Observe the 10-year-old playing with dolls. In 10 years she'll be 20 and may have a real baby of her own to raise.

Look at the 14-year-old eating pizza and laughing with her friends. In 10 years she'll be 24 and working on her Ph.D.

Notice the 18-year-old in his last year of high school. In 10 years he'll be 28 and may be the father of four little ones.

In 10 years will you have made a difference in any one of these lives?

Today

Hebrews 13:8 says, "Jesus Christ is the same yesterday and today and forever."

That's the only thing that remains the same. For everything and everyone else, time moves on and change happens. Nothing is exactly the same as it was yesterday. Either it has deteriorated a little, or it has disappeared completely. That is the way of this physical world we live in. Granted, the change may be almost imperceptible. Still, everything and everyone is changed as today rolls over into tomorrow.

When we stop to consider it clearly, today is all we have. Yesterday is gone. Tomorrow has not come. We live only and always in today.

Yesterday. Both the good and the bad things about yesterday are gone. The pleasures we enjoyed yesterday are memories. The pain we endured has passed. Lessons have been learned. Experience has, hopefully, made us wiser. So we don't look back to regret. Rather, we remember what we learned from yesterday's occurrences that will help us today.

Tomorrow. We can plan for it, but we cannot guarantee it. No amount of worry can ensure that tomorrow will be as we want it to be. Jesus reminded us, "Therefore do not worry about tomorrow, for tomorrow will worry about itself. Each day has enough trouble of its own" (Matthew 6:34).

Yet what we do and who we are today affect tomorrow. Tomorrow is when the consequences for today's wrong actions are realized. Tomorrow is when the rewards for today's right actions pay dividends. Therefore, we need to be intentional and understanding about what we do today so we can see good results tomorrow.

Training

Proverbs 22:6 says, "Train a child in the way he should go, and when he is old he will not turn from it." This is not an ironclad guarantee that our efforts will stop our children from straying from the faith. Rather, it is a principle, a description of the best strategy for passing on the Christian faith.

We all want the best for our families and ourselves in the future. This is natural. It is not a new idea. The phrase "that it may go well" is one that appears, with slight variations, throughout Scripture. It is the rationale behind the admonition to follow God's law in both Deuteronomy and Jeremiah. "Be careful to obey all these regulations I am giving you, so that it may always go well with you and your children after you, because you will be doing what is good and right in the eyes of the LORD your God" (Deuteronomy 12:28). "Walk in all the ways I command you, that it may go well with you" (Jeremiah 7:23). The apostle Paul pointed out that the commandment to honor father and mother was the first one with a promise—"that it may go well with you and that you may enjoy long life on the earth" (Ephesians 6:3). When John wrote to his friend Gaius in his third letter, he expressed the same desire: "I pray that you may enjoy good health and that all may go well with you" (3 John 2).

One way to help (though we cannot guarantee) that "all may go well" is to pass on our Christian faith to the next generation. When we lay down a solid foundation by teaching our children the moral principles of Scripture, we better equip them to face the uncertainties of the future. Training a child in the way he or she should go is building on the foundation of Jesus Christ.

Every athlete knows the value of physical exercise. It is through physical training that athletes prepare themselves for peak performance in their chosen sport. Training for godliness is even more valuable than that. The apostle Paul expressed it like this: "For physical training is of some value, but godliness has value for all things, holding promise for both the present life and the life to come" (1 Timothy 4:8). "The present life" is the today we are concerned about as Christians desiring to pass on the faith to the next generation. "The life to come" is the ultimate future to which all this training leads.

Win as Many as Possible

In these famous verses from 1 Corinthians 9, Paul exhibited an attitude that we can apply to training the next generation.

Though I am free and belong to no man, I make myself a slave to everyone, to win as many as possible. To the Jews I became like a Jew, to win the Jews. To those under the law I became like one under the law (though I myself am not under the law), so as to win those under the law. To those not having the law I became like one not having the law (though I am not free from God's law but am under Christ's law), so as to win those not having the law. To the weak I became weak, to win the weak. I have become all things to all men so that by all possible means I might save some *(vv. 19-22)*.

Paul didn't change the core message of the gospel; he repackaged it to catch their attention. He wasn't a chameleon, changing colors to blend in with the background. He understood his audience and became like them so they could comprehend him. He did none of this for selfish glory, but in order to effectively pass on the Christian faith. "I do all this for the sake of the gospel, that I may share in its blessings" (v. 23).

Paul tried to adapt to every changing situation without compromising the gospel. That is our task as well. To help us in this responsibility, the *Decadal Ministry Guide* has been produced. This booklet lists eight commendable goals along with suggested implementation strategies. Let the following ideas stimulate your own inspirations:

Goal 1: That every church will annually assess the critical issues facing the children and youth in its community.

- *Be aware of what children and youth need, to experience quality of life in all domains (physically, mentally, spiritually, socially, and economically).*
- *Create an assessment device to recognize the critical needs and issues of the children and youth in your community. Possible questions to include are:*
  - ✔ *Is this a need in our church or community?*
  - ✔ *What are we doing to meet this need?*
  - ✔ *What (more) can we do to meet this need?*

Goal 2: That churches will explore the resources available to help them minister to children and youth.

- *Evaluate your current ministry to children and youth. Identify resources available to you: health and welfare, intellectual development, spiritual formation, and social issues.*
- *Identify district personnel with specialized knowledge in various ministry areas, such as those just identified: food programs, after school opportunities, mentoring, tutoring, or family ministry. Contact these persons for individual help.*

Goal 3: That every church will create ministries to meet the needs of children and youth.

- *Research ministry ideas others are doing.*
- *Evaluate those ministries for meeting the needs of children and youth in your church.*

Goal 4: That every church will support and resource the family as a God-ordained structure for nurturing children and youth.

- *Provide materials to highlight the scriptural teachings/understandings about children and youth, especially those that identify parents' responsibility to nurture their children and youth.*
- *Research sources for family ministry books and programs.*
- *Have a family-ministry conference sometime during the decade.*
- *Declare one month as "Home Improvement" month.*
- *Contact the denominational Family Ministries office for current resources about family life.*
- *Provide family-oriented activities, such as:*
  - ✔ *Family photo event. Provide materials for families to make photo-memory books.*
  - ✔ *Family night of prayer.*
  - ✔ *Family bowling tournament.*
  - ✔ *Progressive game night.*
  - ✔ *Cold Turkey Challenge Week. Turn off the TV for a week.*
  - ✔ *Family Life Conference (local church or district-sponsored).*
  - ✔ *Pastoral sermon series.*

Goal 5: That every church will help children and youth identify fully with Christ, helping them enter into a personal relationship with Him.

- *Help the church see the value of children and youth.*
- *Provide resources, such as:*
  - ✔ The Story of Jesus *with accompanying salvation booklet.*

    ✔ *Follow-up materials for evangelistic events.*
    ✔ *Teacher training in the areas of evangelization, spiritual formation, and discipleship.*
    ✔ *Participation in denominational special events for children.*
- Give all children and youth the opportunity to accept Jesus Christ as their Savior.

Goal 6: That all ministries within the church will partner to integrate children and youth into the faith community.

- *Share stories of how children and youth have impacted the kingdom of God; such as, helping parents or others to become Christians or completing ministry projects.*
- *Plan service projects suitable for children and youth and their families.*
- *Provide stewardship materials for children and youth, and encourage stewardship among children and youth.*
- *Relate stories of children and youth in your area who are becoming vital agents of Kingdom work.*

Goal 7: That churches will consider ways to celebrate the significant developmental and spiritual milestones in the lives of children and youth.

- *Affirm milestones and accomplishments of children and youth. Highlight events, such as baby dedications/baptisms, salvation, church membership, and school events.*
- *Provide inexpensive awards and gifts to commemorate special milestones.*

Goal 8: That churches will disciple children and youth.

- *Provide discipleship lessons for children and youth.*
- *Help parents know how to nurture their children and youth spiritually.**

Conclusion

James reminded us of our Christian duty with these words: "Do not merely listen to the word, and so deceive yourselves. Do what it says" (1:22). The call is for each one of us to respond to the love of Christ with some form of service in His kingdom. It is so easy to participate in the services of the church and not be in the service of the King. James calls us to listen to the Word, and then accept the Lord's call to help our weary world.

There are opportunities unlimited, both in and out of the church, for every Christian to find a place of service. Every believer is called to take the message of salvation to his or her world, especially to nurture and shape the next generation of believers. The 7-year-old throwing a baseball in the backyard. The 10-year-old playing with dolls. The 14-year-old eating pizza with her friends. The 18-year-old graduating from high school.

We are called to make a difference in the next 10 years. We are called, not merely to listen, but to act.

Now, having heard that, let's do something!

Notes:

*The *Decadal Ministry Guide* has been produced by the Church of the Nazarene, but it can be useful in other denominations. This brochure and other resources are available at 1-888-644-4510, <childmin@nazarene.org> for E-mail, or at <connecting.nazarene.org> on the Web.

Scriptures: Deuteronomy 12:28; Proverbs 22:6; Jeremiah 7:23; Matthew 6:34; 1 Corinthians 9:19-23; Ephesians 6:3; 1 Timothy 4:8; Hebrews 13:8; James 1:22; 3 John 2